# God's
# Answer to
# Fear, Depression,
# and Discouragement

# God's
# Answer to
# Fear, Depression,
# and Discouragement

# Jimmy Swaggart

**JIMMY SWAGGART MINISTRIES**
P.O. Box 262550 | Baton Rouge, Louisiana 70826-2550
www.jsm.org

ISBN 978-1-941403-24-2
09-133 | COPYRIGHT © 2015 Jimmy Swaggart Ministries®
15 16 17 18 19 20 21 22 23 / EBM / 10 9 8 7 6 5 4 3 2 1

iv

# TABLE OF CONTENTS

# God's
## Answer to
### Fear, Depression,
### and Discouragement

## INTRODUCTION

# INTRODUCTION

THE PROBLEM OF FEAR, depression, and discouragement affects every single human being who has ever lived, even strident believers. However, this doesn't have to be.

The Lord has a solution for this triple malady — a solution that works every single time and rids one of this triplicate problem.

In this book we are going to tell you God's solution and answer to these problems. Please believe me, the Lord has a solution. There is no reason that any believer should be plagued with fear, depression, and discouragement. To be truthful, all of us most definitely have been plagued with these problems, but it's because we do not know and understand what the Word of God says about this terrible difficulty. You can believe me when I state that the Holy Spirit has much to say.

## THE AGE IN WHICH WE LIVE

It is, no doubt, true that the times in which we presently live are stressful, but it doesn't matter how stressful these times are, the Lord is equal to the task. Please believe me, He *is* equal. In other words, there is no single problem that man faces that the Lord doesn't have a solution for it. To be sure, the Lord most definitely has a solution for fear, depression, and discouragement. There is no reason that you as a believer should have one minute of any of these dark shadows that cast their spells over the peace and security of the individual. You are a child of God, and as such, you have a divine protection upon you, about you, and, in fact, all that belongs to you, that is, if you will only function according to the information given in the Word of God.

## THE CROSS OF CHRIST

As you go through this book, you will find that the Cross of Christ is held up as the answer and the solution to man's problems. To be frank, it is not only a solution, it is the only solution, with there being no other. However, we will not just leave that with the statement made that it is the solution, but we will tell you how it is the solution, how that it will bring victory to your heart and to your life, and how that man's dilemma is answered in totality as it regards the Cross of Christ. To be frank, I sense the presence of the Lord even as I dictate these notes.

Unfortunately, most believers begin the Cross and end the Cross at their salvation experience. To be sure, Jesus paid the price at Calvary's Cross for our redemption; however, He also paid the price at Calvary's Cross for our everyday life and living. In other words, the Cross answers every vicissitude of life, every dilemma that life poses for us, every problem that we face, etc. As I've just stated and will state again, I'm going to tell you in this book how the Cross is the solution, and the Cross is the answer. In fact, it is the answer for every problem that man faces, and even those that we think have no solution. Trust me when I tell you that the Cross of Christ is the solution, and the only solution.

In 1997, the Lord spoke graphically to my heart and said the following to me:

- The answer for which you seek is found in the Cross.
- The solution for which you seek is found in the Cross.
- The answer for which you seek is found only in the Cross.

I have found that the Lord meant what He said and, thereby, said what He meant. I found true enough that the answer for which I sought was found in the Cross, and only in the Cross.

## A PERSONAL EXPERIENCE

I will open this book with a personal experience of how that fear can grip an individual to such an extent that it almost paralyzes one. The illustration will take us back to the early 1970s. I think it will prove to be of interest to you.

*Let every tongue Your goodness speak,*
*While Thou sovereign Lord of all,*
*Your strengthening hands uphold the weak,*
*And raise the poor who fall.*

*When sorrows bow the spirit down,*
*When virtue lies distressed;*
*Beneath the proud oppressor's frown,*
*You give the mourner rest.*

*You know the pains Your servants feel,*
*You hear Your children's cry,*
*And their best wishes to fulfill,*
*Your grace is ever nigh.*

*Your mercy never shall remove,*
*From men of heart sincere;*
*You save the souls whose humble love,*
*Is joined with holy fear.*

*My lips shall dwell upon Your praise,*
*And spread Your fame abroad:*
*Let all the sons of Adam raise,*
*The honors of their God.*

# God's
## Answer to
### Fear, Depression,
### and Discouragement

# A PERSONAL EXPERIENCE

# A PERSONAL EXPERIENCE

HEAT VAPORS RISING OFF the macadam surface of the landing strip caused the horizon to sway and undulate as we shaded our eyes and stared off toward the end of the runway. We had flown to the sleepy little town of Lake Providence, Louisiana, after lunch and spent the afternoon with Frances' sister, Peggy Messenger. Now we were heading home.

With several hours to bake in the sun, the metal wing surface of the Cessna 310 was almost painful to the touch as we clambered across it to slip into the cabin. Things weren't much better inside. Airplanes aren't like automobiles. They don't have huge expanses of windows that can be rolled down to provide air circulation. Airplanes are designed to be comfortable in flight. A parked airplane rapidly becomes a furnace.

Having completed the preflight inspection before we entered the plane, I hastened through the checklist. I hit the primer switch and watched as the needle climbed upward. When it reached the green, I punched the red button that brought to life the first of the 285 horsepower continental engines. It responded faithfully, and a moment later, I was repeating the procedure for the other engine. We felt a welcomed change in the cabin temperature as we started taxiing toward the end of the strip. Here we paused while I ran the engines up and checked out the magnetos to make sure we were protected by the double ignition system that makes aircraft engines so reliable. With mags okay, we settled back with the nose of the plane headed down the white line marking the center of the runway.

I eased the twin throttles forward and felt the pressure of the acceleration press me back into the seat. Because of the heat, the air was thin. Because of the thinness of the air, it would take more speed than usual to support the weight of the aircraft. This meant that we would use the major part of the 3,000-foot runway before we had built up enough speed for the plane to fly.

## AIRBORNE

As the airspeed indicator went past the critical point of 80 knots, (80 nautical miles per hour), a smile flitted across my face. Every takeoff rewards the pilot with a momentary flash of accomplishment as he finds himself with flying speed and unused runway ahead of him. With no need to lift off prematurely, I allowed myself the luxury of holding her down while I built up surplus flying speed. Finally, as the needle swept past 95, I eased the yoke back, and the nimble Cessna leaped effortlessly into the air.

As we cleared the ground, I punched at the little wheel-shaped switch that activates the landing gear motor. With the plane "cleaned up" and offering less resistance to the passage of air over its surface, our speed increased as I eased into a left turn and headed out across the lake and toward the Mississippi River. It would act as our road map back to Baton Rouge, Louisiana. It had been a routine day. I had no premonition that within a matter of minutes this flight would be seared into my brain with a clarity that would never allow me to forget it. Frances sat looking idly out the right window lost in her own thoughts as we climbed to 5,000 feet. At that altitude, I snapped on the autopilot, a black box that would allow me to sit back and become a passenger as the electronic circuitry took over the job of maintaining the speed, direction, and altitude of the plane.

It was a deceptively peaceful moment as we bore on southward. The twists and turns of the Mississippi River carried it first to the right of us and then to the left. Off in the distance to the left, I could make out Vicksburg, Mississippi, the sight of one of the great battles of the Civil War. A little further on would be Natchez, and shortly after that, Baton Rouge. The crops and fields laid out in checkerboard patterns were logical and ordered, a treat to the eye.

I love flying. In fact, in those days I spent a great deal of time in the air going to crusades. I wasn't able to spend nearly as much time as I would have liked in the pilot's seat. What little time I could steal, however, to actually hold the wheel in my hand and captain the plane was time that instilled a feeling no other human activity can produce. I am very grateful to the Lord that He allowed me to learn to fly, even though that's been a long time ago, and I no longer indulge my likes and dislikes in that capacity at present, and have not for a long, long time.

## THE STORM

Interstate 20 cuts across Vicksburg and crosses the Mississippi River, and I momentarily broke my reverie as I unconsciously added it to the mental progress chart I was keeping. Then I frowned as my eyes swept back again to the horizon.

Directly ahead, the sky was no longer blue. An ominous darkening had replaced the sapphire clarity, and jagged streaks of lightning were cutting fiery slashes across the dark wall that completely obscured the horizon to the right. That, of course, wasn't too bad a sign. As the weather was moving in from the right (from the west), the speed of our plane should allow me to slip past the weather front before it reached our pathway along the river.

However, then my confidence ebbed as I swept my eyes off to the left. There, too, I could detect a buildup of darkening cloud masses and unless my eyes were deceiving me, lightning was playing around within these, too. A go/no-go decision would have to be made fairly soon.

I weighed the factors. Unquestionably, things looked ominous off to the right and the left, but I could see Natchez ahead of me with no difficulty. Also, there seemed to be a clear path of reasonable weather pointing directly along the route the plane was headed.

I adjusted the little wheel on the autopilot and watched as the nose of the plane dipped to take us lower where we might be able to pass under the worst of the turbulence if we should inadvertently wander into something more than I wanted to challenge. Hopefully though, we would find ourselves back in Baton Rouge in about 45 minutes with nothing more than the inconvenience of clothing dampened by light rain as we walked from the plane to the car. I decided to press on. It would be a mistake.

By the time we drew abreast of Natchez, Mississippi, our altitude had decreased to about 1,500 feet. I am very familiar with the area, so I wasn't concerned about towers, hills, or other obstacles. The only possible danger lay in the glowering pinnacles of black clouds beginning to impinge on our alley through to Baton Rouge.

When I decided to continue our flight, I mentally calculated that we had more than enough time to clear the closing fingers of the two storm centers as they moved eastward. But now, enticed within the nutcracker jaws of the two occluding menaces by the hope that we would squeeze through before they collided, I realized I was mistaken. They weren't two sequential fronts moving along at the same pace, but two separate fronts approaching each other from opposite directions. We were in trouble!

Shortly after passing Natchez, the first few drops of water splattered against the windshield. The rain rapidly increased though to the point where there was a solid buildup of water laying across the windshield. I was as blind as if the whole cabin had been wrapped in opaque material. I lost all reference to the ground, the horizon, and anything else that would help to give me a bearing on our situation.

I immediately dialed 123.0 (Approach Control in Baton Rouge) to see what the weather was there and to ask for a radar vector to lead us in. However, apparently the interference of the lightning within the storm was blanketing my signal. I could hear them, but they couldn't hear me.

I thank God that I had the training and ability to fly the plane in just about any condition, even though I did not have the certification to do so. Not being instrument rated though, it was now legally required to perform a one-eighty.

This involved swinging the plane onto a course directly opposite the heading that brought us into instrument conditions. Thus, at least in theory, you head back into clear weather. Fixing my eyes on the gauges and needles that gave me the only indication of our attitude in relation to the earth, I prepared to do just that.

By the time I had swung around and had us headed back in the direction of Natchez, we were down to 800 feet, not a large margin for error in a high performance aircraft like a Cessna 310. Frances was sitting quietly, and even though I couldn't remove my eyes from the instrument panel to see what she was doing, I was sure she was praying.

All the things my various flight instructors had taught me began to flood into my conscious level.

Keep calm. Keep cool. Your first responsibility is to fly the plane.

The engines are dependable. Don't waste your time looking for imaginary problems with them. Having taken control of the plane from the autopilot and reversed our course, I hoped for an almost immediate improvement in the visibility. There wasn't any. The blanket of water that lay opaquely across the windshield was as impenetrable as ever. For the first time, I began to feel the icy fingers of panic and fear probing at my innermost parts.

Someone might well ask, "Did you pray?"

No, I really didn't. In all honesty, I reacted just as most people do when they are in an emergency situation. I was too busy fighting panic and trying to retain control of the situation to even think about praying.

So, I didn't consciously pray at that time. My eyes were rapidly scanning back and forth over the various dials and needles that gave me our only indication of what our situation was.

The average non-flyer may not realize it, but once visual contact with the ground is lost, there is no way in the world to tell for sure what your relationship is to the earth. A pilot without visual contact can sit, comfortable and confident, while his plane goes into a long spiraling dive that will see it plummet into the ground nose first.

Without a compass (or even with one if it isn't watched carefully), the plane will wander off course in a matter of seconds. So, my hands were full monitoring the information supplied to me by the various needles and gauges before me. I thanked God in that moment for the hours I had been able to spend practicing blind flying under simulated blind conditions "under the hood." This training was the only thing that now stood between Frances and me and violent death.

## FEAR

Things were proceeding along all right. The turn and bank indicators said we were on a straight course. The artificial horizon testified that we were upright and level. The altimeter said we had plenty of air between us and contact with the ground. I should have been able to relax and wait patiently until we ran out of the blinding torrent that filled the entirety of our immediate environment, but fear was threatening to take over my body and render me incapable of performing the very tasks that had to be performed if we were to survive the present emergency.

The first indication I had that things weren't as they should be was a lump that suddenly appeared in my throat. I tried time after time to swallow it, but it stubbornly refused to go down. It felt like a golf ball embedded in the bottom of my esophagus.

This was a physical manifestation of fear taking control of my body. In the beginning I had been able to control any tendency toward fear. Now though, I was reaching the limits of my ability to keep my own body under control.

My right leg started to jerk spastically on the rudder

pedal. I willed it to stop, but the jerking only grew worse. With the chore of monitoring the various instruments and maintaining a delicate touch on the controls, the last thing I needed was a recalcitrant body to demand my attention. I hammered at my knee with a clenched fist in an effort to bring it into subjection. It went right on jerking anyway.

Adding to my concern over the mechanics of keeping the plane in the air was my desire to keep from Frances the true import of the situation. I knew that she knew we were in trouble. I knew that she was praying. I also knew that she was sufficiently knowledgeable in the matter of airplanes to know that I had my hands full and was near the limits of my capability.

In a situation like this, a moment seems like an hour and an hour seems like eternity. Even though I had done the prescribed one-eighty, and I knew we were headed back to where the weather should be better, the time seemed to go on endlessly as we seemed to be suspended motionless in a sea of raging turbulence, impenetrable water, and slashing bursts of lightning.

After what seemed to be interminable hours, we suddenly broke out into the clear. Towering walls of black, lightning-laced clouds hung over us on all sides except one. Thankfully, that was the direction slightly to the right of the nose of the plane — the direction in which I could see Natchez.

We were now out of physical danger from the storm, but we weren't yet safe. It actually took an effort of will for me to maintain my concentration as I took the plane through the pattern and then touched it down gently on the Natchez airport strip.

I parked the plane near the gas pump and told the line boy to fill the tanks as I knew we wouldn't be able to go on any further that day. And then, as I approached the counter in the operations office of the flight base, a strange thing happened. I suddenly felt as if all the bones had been removed from my body. The room went dark, and the counter swam before my eyes. The voice of the line boy sounded far away as he told me the amount I owed him for the fuel. If I hadn't gripped the counter edge with all my strength, I would have collapsed on the floor. This whole experience demonstrated something that is all too often true when we allow ourselves to fall prey to fear. At no time during the whole episode were we in danger because of factors beyond our control. The airplane performed admirably. The engines never faltered. Every gauge in control performed its function without hesitation. However, there was one faulty piece of equipment aboard, and that one weak and inefficient device almost cost us our lives.

If I had undertaken the flight with an instructor aboard, and he had suddenly snapped down the visor on my hood and said, "You've just run into instrument conditions, make a one-eighty and return to Natchez," I could have done it with no problem whatsoever.

However, this wasn't a training exercise. This was reality. There was real water sluicing across the windshield. It was real lightning dancing and crashing around us on all sides.

This fact shouldn't have made any difference. The necessary actions are the same whether its reality or training.

The one thing that made the difference was fear. Fear put me under unbearable pressure, threatened my performance, and actually began to influence my physical body. Fear and fear alone came close to putting Frances and me in our graves years before the Lord meant for us to be there.

> *I can see far down the mountain,*
> *Where I've wandered many years,*
> *Often hindered on my journey,*
> *By ghosts of doubts and fears,*
> *Broken vows and disappointments,*
> *Thickly strewn along the way,*
> *But the Spirit led unerring,*
> *To the land I hold today.*

# God's
## Answer to
### Fear, Depression,
### and Discouragement

# CHAPTER 2

## THE SPIRIT OF FEAR

# THE SPIRIT OF FEAR

IN II TIMOTHY 1:7, we are told, *"For God has not given us the spirit of fear; but of power, and of love, and of a sound mind."*

In Paul's second letter to Timothy (and his last one we might quickly add), the Holy Spirit through the apostle tells us a great deal in just a few words. The term "the spirit of fear" is used here. I believe this refers to an actual conscious being, a personality, a demon power that concentrates its attention in this particular area.

One brother made the statement sometime ago that this couldn't be so — that this couldn't be a specific spirit of fear — because if it were, the terms *power, love,* and *a sound mind* would also have to be spirits.

In actuality, I think he was right and wrong at the same time. In my opinion he was wrong when he said the phrase "spirit of fear" is just a term and not a reference to a specific personality. However, I think he was right when he said that power, love, and a sound mind also have to be of a spirit. In fact, they emanate from the Holy Spirit.

There is a demon spirit involved in the spirit of fear, and the Holy Spirit is involved in the power, the love, and the sound mind. These things proceed forth from the Holy Spirit. The spirit of fear proceeds from Satan.

In I Kings 22:21 and 22, we are told of a demon spirit who appeared before the Lord and offered to serve as a *"lying spirit."* Yes, there are demon spirits in heaven; however, they will be expelled soon (Rev. 12:7-9).

In I Samuel 28:7, we find mention of a *"familiar spirit,"* which is a spirit that knows hidden things about people and tells these to the medium with whom it works.

Paul mentions *"seducing spirits"* in I Timothy 4:1.

Jesus spoke of unclean spirits many times.

So, there is sound basis for believing that there is, in fact, a spirit of fear. It is a diabolical, demonic spirit that is charged by Lucifer, which is causing havoc, trouble, heartache, and physical illness. It even causes death in the lives of countless people — even Christians.

## RESPECT

If we are to understand fear as an entity, we must first understand that there are actually several different ways in which the word *fear* may be defined or understood. The spirit of fear has already been mentioned briefly. However, the word *fear* in the context of respect is something completely different from fear when viewed within the meaning of panic, anxiety, depression, and worry.

Fear in the context of respect is a normal, helpful, and God-given emotion. If God in His wisdom hadn't seen fit to equip us with the ability to feel fear, none of us would probably live beyond our fifth or sixth birthday. In the normal meaning of the word, fear (respect) protects us from involving ourselves in activities that could be dangerous to us. As such, fear is really one of the most valuable of the many emotions given to us by God.

A child soon learns that if he puts his finger into the fire, he will be burned. After this, he doesn't really fear the fire, but he does respect the fire. Likewise, children learn that they can't play on the highway where they might be run over by a truck or car. This is a normal, healthy awareness of a situation that holds danger when dealt with foolishly. As such, fear is an invaluable tool in protecting us from dangers that should be avoided by a prudent individual.

It is often said of people who demonstrate an unusual amount of courage that they doesn't know the meaning of the word *fear.*

Actually, if someone didn't know the meaning of the word *fear,* he would be mentally deranged and a great threat to himself (and probably to society in general). If that phrase were true, all it would imply is that the person in question didn't have sense enough to recognize danger well enough to protect himself.

## FEAR GOD

We are told any number of places in the Word of God to

fear God. In Joshua 24:14 we are told, *"Now therefore fear the* LORD*, and serve Him in sincerity and in truth."*

Does this mean that we should approach our Lord and our God cringing and cowering like a stray dog? Hardly. This means very simply that we should respect God. We are to be well aware that He is all-powerful, but at the same time, we should realize that He is also all-loving.

When Joshua delivered these words, he was in no way setting up a contradiction between this statement and the latter one in I John 4:18, where it states, *"There is no fear in love; but perfect love casts out fear."*

John is talking about the spirit of fear. Joshua, on the other hand, is referring to the beneficial, rational realization that God has the potential power to deal with us severely if we fail to deal with Him properly! As such, it is only intelligent to fear God, that is, to recognize His capabilities that are unending and respect Him for these capabilities. The important point to be made is this: There is no contradiction between these two statements. One refers to the normal, healthy, and helpful emotion given to us by God to help us through life. The other refers to a malignant, corrosive, and completely harmful process that is not God-given, but is rather fathered by the ultimate author of harm and hate for mankind — Satan himself.

Fear is perhaps the most destructive force at work in the world today. Is that statement overdrawn? Yes. The atomic bomb represents fantastic destructive potential, but it is potential. Fear on the other hand is being utilized daily by its author, who is Satan. As such, fear is an actual working force that is destroying lives by the untold thousands at the very moment that we hold this book. It is this destructive fear, the one represented by the spirit of fear, that this book will deal in the main.

## THE MIND

The mind of man is the gateway to the spirit of man. When the Bible uses the term *heart,* it is not speaking of the physical organ beating within our breasts, but is rather speaking of the spirit and the soul of man. The spirit and the soul are the real you, but the mind is the gateway to the spirit. In other words, this is where Satan first plants his thoughts — the mind. Before sin is carried out, it is conceived in the mind. It is so easy to look at circumstances, problems, difficulties, and such like and allow our minds to become seized by the disposition of helplessness or even hopelessness, i.e., fear, which then pulls the trigger of oppression. If this happens, we know it's not God doing it, but it's our own minds that are not properly settled in Christ. In such a climate, there is plenty of room for one's mind to imagine all sorts of things, hence, fear is a disposition of the mind.

## THE CROSS OF CHRIST

First of all, I'm going to take you to the Cross. The believer must understand and accept at face value that what

Jesus did at the Cross answers every question, addresses every problem, and shows us the solution to every difficulty. In other words, what Jesus did at the Cross is the answer, and the only answer, to man's dilemma.

Most Christians have a working knowledge of the Cross of Christ as it refers to our salvation. "Jesus died for me" is perhaps the greatest statement that any human being could ever begin to make, but that's as far as it goes with most. They don't understand the part the Cross plays as it regards our sanctification — how we live for God on a daily basis, how we grow in grace and the knowledge of the Lord, and how we have victory over the world, the flesh, and the Devil. In fact, most believers have never heard the statements that you have just read. Now, we must understand that the Cross of Christ is just as much involved, and even more so, in our sanctification as it was our justification.

First of all, please understand that 90 percent or more of what Paul gave us in his 14 epistles has to do with the Cross of Christ relative to our sanctification and not our justification. While He most definitely deals with justification, the greater thrust by far is sanctification — how we live for God. The simple fact is that most believers simply don't know how to live for God. I realize that's quite a statement, but regrettably, it happens to be true.

As a believer, you are to place your faith consistently in the Cross of Christ as it regards your daily living for God, and maintain your faith exclusively in Christ and His finished work. That's the key — your faith. However, your faith must have the correct object, and that correct object is Jesus Christ and Him crucified (Rom. 6:3-5; 8:1-11; I Cor. 1:17-18, 23; 2:2; Col. 2:10-15).

Please note the following points very carefully:

- Jesus Christ is the source of all things that we receive from God (Jn. 1:1-3, 14, 29; 14:6).
- The Cross of Christ is the means, and the only means, by which all of these wonderful things are given to us (I Cor. 1:17-18, 23; 2:2).
- With Christ as our source and the Cross as the means, the object of our faith must be the Cross of Christ, and we aren't speaking of the wooden beam on which He died, but rather what He there accomplished (Gal. 6:14; Col. 2:10-15).
- With Christ as our source and the Cross of Christ our means, the Holy Spirit, who works exclusively within the boundaries of the Cross of Christ, will then work mightily on our behalf.

Above all, Satan doesn't want the believer to know this which I am giving you right now. He was defeated at Calvary's Cross along with all of his principalities, powers, demon spirits, fallen angels, etc. That's the reason he doesn't want you to know the things that we are now giving you. The Cross is the answer, and it is the only answer.

### HOW DO I KEEP EVIL THOUGHTS OUT OF MY MIND?

I suppose that through the years I have been asked that

question maybe more than any other. There is a way that you can keep evil thoughts out of your mind, and let me give it to you.

Nearly 2,800 years ago, the great prophet Isaiah gave us this particular word. He said:

*"To appoint unto them who mourn in Zion, to give unto them beauty for ashes, the oil of joy for mourning, the garment of praise for the spirit of heaviness; that they might be called trees of righteousness, the planting of the LORD, that He might be glorified"* (Isa. 61:3).

As we have stated, sin begins in the heart but quickly goes to the mind, and then the sin, fear, etc., is carried out. I'm going to show you how to stop that.

In this tremendous word that the great prophet gave us, there is a phrase in the Scripture that I want you to notice. It says:

*"To give unto them ... The garment of praise for the spirit of heaviness."*

Two things are said, and we will deal with the latter one first.

*"The spirit of heaviness"* is demonic oppression, and fear, even abject fear, always accompanies demonic oppression. It's as if 200 pounds are on the person's shoulder. It's as if the sun has been hidden from view, and there is nothing but darkness. It's as if there is no way out, and it seems that there is no solution to the problem. That's the reason the Holy Spirit called it *"the spirit of heaviness."*

Every single believer who has ever lived has experienced

this spirit of heaviness more than one time to be sure. Let me get back to the Cross for a moment.

## THE VICTORY OF THE CROSS

A short time ago on a Sunday morning, I was preaching to our people at Family Worship Center. I was dealing with this spirit of oppression — this spirit of heaviness. While I was preaching, all of a sudden something came to me. In 1997, the Lord gave me the great word of the Cross and how it works in the hearts and lives of believers. To be sure, it has revolutionized my life and my ministry.

As I was preaching, it suddenly dawned on me that since that great word of the Cross was given to me, I have not experienced one moment of demonic oppression — not one moment of this spirit of heaviness. As I dictate this, that has been some 18 years ago.

Now I want to tell you how to keep evil thoughts out of your mind, which can lead to all types of problems. As we have stated, Satan plants his thoughts in your mind at the beginning. They then go to your soul and your spirit, which are then carried out through your physical body. So, let's see how that we can close up the mind to that which is ungodly and keep it open to that which is godly.

The great prophet told us of the garment of praise. What did he mean by that?

First of all, a garment is something we wear, and the Holy Spirit through Isaiah is telling us that we should wear a garment of praise. What do I mean by that?

## THE GARMENT OF PRAISE

In your daily duties, as it comes to your mind, just start to praise the Lord. You don't have to do it out loud. Actually, you can do it under your breath to where no one can hear you, but you just start praising Him and thanking Him for all that He's done for you. Tell Him how much you love Him and keep doing it until your mind goes to something else, which it will very shortly. Then, the next moment when your mind snaps back to the Lord, begin to praise Him again. Just keep doing it.

You will find that you will subconsciously start to praise the Lord without even thinking about it. Please understand that as you do this, it will never get old. You will sense a euphoric spirit of joy that will fill your heart and fill your soul, but here's the main thing: There will be no place for evil thoughts, no place for doubt and unbelief, no place for fear, no place for depression, and no place for discouragement. You are praising the One who can do all things.

The reason the Holy Spirit refers to it as *"a garment of praise"* is because you are to wear this thing like you do a garment. That means that it covers your spirit, and it covers your soul. Every time you think about it and begin to praise the Lord, no room is left for fear and depression.

What I have just given to you is that which the Lord has given to me, and it has revolutionized my life and my thinking.

It has given me a peace that passes all understanding, and it is so wonderful that I want you to have it, as well, and you most definitely can.

*Amazing grace, how sweet the sound,*
*That saved a wretch like me,*
*I once was lost, but now I'm found,*
*Was blind but now I see.*

# God's Answer to Fear, Depression, and Discouragement

CHAPTER 3

## THE WORD OF GOD

# THE WORD OF GOD

THE PSALMIST SAID:

*"He who dwells in the secret place of the Most High* (in the finished work of Christ) *shall abide under the shadow of the Almighty* (under His protection)."

He then said, *"I will say of the LORD, He is my refuge and my fortress: my God; in Him will I trust."*

We must not forget this part: *"Surely He shall deliver you from the snare of the fowler* (plans of hurt and destruction made by Satan), *and from the noisome pestilence."*

And finally, *"He shall cover you with His feathers, and under His wings shall you trust: His truth shall be your shield and buckler.*

*"You shall not be afraid* (no fear) *for the terror by night; nor for the arrow that flies by day"* (Ps. 91:1-5).

In other words, Satan will try, but he won't make any headway.

In the last chapter, I gave you the solution to fear, depression, and discouragement, but I want to go into more detail as to how the Holy Spirit through the Word of God deals with these problems.

When the believer anchors himself in the Cross of Christ and takes full advantage of the garment of praise, he will find quickly that this guarantees all the benefits of the atonement. The Holy Spirit then goes to work on his behalf and always does great and mighty things. That is the secret of our protection, our guidance, our strength, and our ability — the Holy Spirit. However, as we've said over and over again, the Holy Spirit works exclusively within the parameters of the finished work of Christ, i.e., the Cross, which must always be the object of our faith.

Beautifully enough, love is the antidote for fear (I Jn. 4:18).

When one properly understands the Cross, one has a tendency to understand the love of God much more because the Cross is the greatest example of the love of God that man has ever known or ever will know.

So, my contention is this: That which will inspire trust, confidence, and faith is a proper understanding of the Cross and our proper faith in that great sacrifice. This gives us the help of the Holy Spirit, which we will address to a greater degree momentarily, who gives us all assurance, which drives out all fear. Considering that this is one of the most powerful emotions with which believers have to contend, let's look at the situation to a greater degree.

## FEAR AS AN EMOTION

Old Testament uses of fear often indicate the all-too-familiar feeling of terror. Adam and Eve fled from God in the garden of Eden, with Adam later exclaiming, *"I heard Your voice in the garden, and I was afraid, because I was naked"* (Gen. 3:10).

A basic cause of this emotion is awareness of vulnerability because of sin or because of the perceived power of another to do harm. The Hebrew people experienced such terror at Sinai (Deut. 5:5), and Saul was gripped by fear when he saw the size of the massive Philistine army (I Sam. 28:5).

The antidote for the emotion of fear is the conviction that God is for us and with us. This conviction is cemented, as stated, by a proper understanding of the Cross of Christ. Understanding that, one cannot help but know that God is for us and with us.

I realize that many would say that they know that anyhow; however, I maintain that once the believer has a proper understanding of the Cross as he should have, then he will really know this of which we speak. It's impossible for most believers to compare this of which I say for the simple reason that most have never known the assurance that a proper understanding of the Cross brings.

Of course, in Old Testament times, there would not have really been a knowledge of the Cross — only the assurance that God was with them.

Consequently, Moses exhorted Israel:

*"And shall say unto them, Hear, O Israel, you approach this day unto battle against your enemies: let not your hearts faint, fear not, and do not tremble, neither be you terrified because of them; For the* LORD *your God is He*

*who goes with you, to fight for you against your enemies, to save you"* (Deut. 20:3-4).

There are many situations in which fear is appropriate. We should never berate ourselves because of our fears, providing we know what to do with them. David recorded a time of personal fear in Psalm 56. In that psalm he presents fear as an opportunity rather than a weakness. It is only when we are afraid that we can experience the meaning of trust in God.

David traces his own emotions and shows a pattern that we can duplicate.

He said:

*"What time I am afraid, I will trust in You. In God I will praise His Word* (the garment of praise), *in God I have put my trust; I will not fear what flesh can do unto me"* (Ps. 56:3-4).

The pattern is this:

- David experiences fear.
- He turns to God with a statement of trust.
- He recalls God's self-revelation in the Word.
- He determines not to anticipate evil, for He knows that God is in control, and no mere mortal or satanic spirit can overcome the Lord.

We must not allow fear to become a disposition of our minds simply because as a believer (I'll say it again), we know that God is in control.

Now that we have the Cross and all the victory it has afforded, there is really no reason for a believer to allow fear to overcome him in any capacity.

## FEAR OF ANTICIPATED EVIL

When Paul wrote, *"For God has not given us the spirit of fear; but of power, and of love, and of a sound mind"* (II Tim. 1:7), he was actually warning Timothy about the fear of anticipated evil.

Many passages in the Word of God portray the emotion of fear as a rouse by an intellectual anticipation of what might happen. At times such anticipation does not create actual terror, but it does find expression in worry or anxiety, which is not a very pleasant state.

Abraham was afraid to say "she is my wife," for he anticipated that the local ruler of the Philistines might want Sarah for himself because she was so beautiful. Abraham was afraid the ruler of the Philistines might murder him to get her (Gen. 26:7).

When Moses was told by God to return to Egypt to lead Israel to freedom (Ex., Chpts. 3-4), he raised many objections. Moses anticipated all sorts of problems that might arise, and his actions made it clear that he was afraid.

The antidote to such fear of anticipated evil is found in looking to the Lord with trust, but now, and I speak of the time after the Cross, the believer can experience trust in a much greater fashion. With the Cross now being a fact, it portrays to all concerned exactly what God has done for us — meaning that every power of darkness has been defeated. As well, and I will mention it again:

If you as a believer will start praising the Lord every

time your mind thinks of Him, you will see fear begin to disappear. Begin to extol His greatness and glory and begin to thank Him for all the good things He has done, is doing, and will do. You don't even have to say this out loud; you can say it under your breath to where it can be heard by no one but yourself and the Lord. You should do that every time your mind comes to the Lord.

Very soon your mind will go to something else because it's impossible to think on two things at once. However, every time (and I stress every time that your mind comes to the Lord) begin praising Him, and you will find that fear will leave, doubt will leave, unbelief will leave, discouragement will leave, oppression will leave, depression will leave, etc.

Psalm 112 celebrates the blessings given to the person who honors and remembers God. It goes right along with what I've been saying about praising the Lord constantly.

*"He shall not be afraid of evil tidings: his heart is fixed, trusting in the LORD. His heart is established, he shall not be afraid, until he see his desire upon his enemies"* (Ps. 112:7-8).

If believers in the Old Testament could be encouraged to have such trust in God, how much more should we today practice such trust, and even on a much greater scale. In fact, the New Testament believer operates on a much different basis than the Old Testament believer.

All of these great blessings of which we now speak were then only in shadow and were not easy to come by. Now, we have a completed covenant, which is also an everlasting covenant (Heb. 13:20). This covenant is all wrapped up in what Jesus did at the Cross and in His resurrection.

## WHAT GOD HAS DONE

Before the Cross, the old covenant concerned what God would do. The new covenant now concerns what God has done. Something to be done and something already done are two different things altogether.

It is certainly true that God's word could be depended on. What He said would be done definitely would be brought to pass; however, until it was done, the great victory promised could not actually be attained, at least not in totality.

God who commands events in His universe is in control of each believer's future. Whatever trials the future may hold, the person whose trust is in the Lord will have hope and a sense of personal security.

And yet, I say again that this hope and personal security are properly understood presently only as the believer has a proper understanding of the Cross and his place in the finished work of Christ. Unfortunately, precious few have that understanding.

## FEAR OF THE LORD

Every believer should have a healthy fear of the Lord; however, this is not a slavish or craven fear, but something else altogether.

If the believer has a proper fear of God, this will also have mastered ordinary human fears.

Such fear is reverence for God. We who fear God recognize Him as the ultimate reality, and we respond to Him accordingly. Fear of God is called *"the beginning of knowledge"* (Prov. 1:7), meaning that taking God into account is the foundation of a disciplined and holy life (Gen. 20:11; Ps. 36:1-4; Prov. 1:3).

To fear God means to reject every competing power and to serve Him only (Deut. 6:13). Fear of the Lord is expressed by walking in all His ways, by loving Him, and by serving Him with all your heart and soul (Deut. 10:12; Job 1:1; Ps. 128:1).

While fear of God is closely linked with morality and with obedience to God's commands, it also has a freeing quality as well. To fear God means to recognize Him as creator and to know that His plans stand firm forever (Ps. 33:8-11).

God has a special concern for all who fear Him (Ps. 31:19; 34:9). Thus, those who fear God can say with the psalmist:

*"Our soul waits for the* LORD: *He is our help and our shield.*

*"For our heart shall rejoice in Him, because we have trusted in His holy name.*

*"Let Your mercy, O* LORD, *be upon us, according as we hope in You"* (Ps. 33:20-22).

## THE BEHAVIORAL IMPACT OF FEAR

The Old Testament points out that those who fear God show their awareness of who He is by their moral choices as well as by their worship. The New Testament helps us to further explore ways that fear shapes human behavior.

The enemies of Jesus are portrayed several times holding back their hatred and resisting the impulse to attack Him for fear of the crowds who thought Him to be at least a prophet (Mat. 21:46; Mk. 12:12).

On the other hand, some who believed in Jesus were afraid (man fear) and so would not acknowledge Him openly (Jn. 7:13; 12:42). King Herod wanted to execute John the Baptist, but he held back for a time out of fear of the people (Mat. 14:5). Even Peter so feared the members of the circumcision party in Jerusalem who came to visit the new Gentile church in Antioch that he stopped eating with the non-Jewish believers (Gal. 2:12).

Each of these instances involves a fear of what others will think or how they will react to us. Such fear is a primary source of conformity in society. However, Jesus told His disciples to put this kind of fear behind them, even if some would hate them because of Him (Mat. 10:26).

We are to be in awe of God, not of people, for He alone holds the ultimate power (Mat. 10:28; Lk. 12:4). Such fear of the Lord releases us from bondage to the opinions of others and frees us to act spontaneously and to choose what is right.

So, Jesus taught us not to be afraid even of those who seem to have the power to kill. God is in control of even the sparrow's fall, and He told them, *"You are of more value than many sparrows"* (Mat. 10:30-31; Lk. 12:7). When we are aware of God's power and of His love, we are released from those lesser terrors that might move us to compromise or to disobey the Lord.

## FEAR OF GOD'S WORKING

We can understand the amazement and the initial fright that overtook those who first observed Jesus' miracles. In some cases, fear was transformed to adoration as bystanders praised God for what Jesus had done (Lk. 5:26). However, all too often we see a reaction.

In Gadara, Jesus released a demon-possessed man and sent the hoard of evil spirits that had dominated him into a herd of pigs. The people saw their neighbor sitting there dressed and in his right mind, and *"they were afraid"* (Mk. 5:15). Because of this they began to plead with Jesus to leave their region. They were uncomfortable with God's work, even though His power had been used for good — even great good.

When Felix, the Roman governor in Caesarea, listened to Paul speak about faith in Christ and the coming judgment, he was afraid (Acts 24:25). Felix sent Paul away from him.

John helps us to understand such reactions, which are so much like the reaction of Adam and Eve in Eden. John said that light has come into the world, but men love darkness instead of light because their deeds are evil. Everyone who does evil hates the light and will not come into the light for fear that his deeds will be exposed (Jn. 3:19-20).

Man's reaction to God's action and to God's Word is often to reject them or to try to flee from God. Sin has so warped our perception that God's love is difficult to see. Instead, an often unacknowledged sense of guilt creates in us a fear of exposure and leads us to flee headlong from the only source of healing.

*My Lord has garments so wondrous fine,*
*And myrrh their texture fills.*
*Its fragrance reached to this heart of mine,*
*With joy my being thrills.*

*Out of the ivory palaces,*
*Into a world of woe,*
*Only His great eternal love,*
*Made my Saviour go.*

*His life had also its sorrows sore,*
*For aloes had a part;*
*And when I think of the Cross He bore,*
*My eyes with teardrops start.*

*His garments too were in cassia dipped,*
*With healing in a touch:*
*Each time my feet in some sin have slipped,*
*He took me from its clutch."*

*In garments glorious He will come,*
*To open wide the doors;*
*And I shall enter my heavenly home,*
*To dwell forevermore.*

# God's Answer to Fear, Depression, and Discouragement

## FEAR IN THE BELIEVER'S RELATIONSHIP WITH GOD

CHAPTER FOUR

# FEAR IN THE BELIEVER'S
# RELATIONSHIP WITH GOD

TWO THEMES CONCERNING FEAR are found in the New Testament. The first is a reflection of the Old Testament's presentation of the fear of the Lord as reverent awe, which we have briefly addressed. This attitude is still wholly appropriate for believers.

When Ananias and Sapphira lied to the Holy Spirit and immediately died, this kind of fear gripped the Jerusalem church and all who heard about these events (Acts 5:11). Acts reports that immediately there was renewed spiritual vitality that generated healings and stimulated evangelism (Acts 5:12-16).

Peter calls us to remember the holiness of God and the fact that God judges each man's work impartially. Being aware of who God is and being in awe of Him, we are to live our lives as strangers here in reverent fear (I Pet. 1:17; 2:17).

While this theme of a reverent awe as being an appropriate fear of the Lord is found in the New Testament, there is a second theme — one that stresses release from fear. Paul reminds us that the Spirit, whom we received at conversion (actually the Scripture of our study), does not make us a slave again to fear. Instead, the Spirit testifies to our sonship. As children, we can approach God confidently and call on Him as Father (Rom. 8:15).

John adds this thought:

*"There is no fear in love; but perfect love casts out fear: because fear has torment. He who fears is not made perfect in love"* (I Jn. 4:18).

The impact of the statements of both Paul and John is to purify our concept of spiritual fear. The Old Testament concept of the fear of God must be understood in the context of covenant relationship with God.

## FEAR AND FAITH

We experience fear as fright and also as anxiety about what might happen in the future. In fact, this latter type of fear is the greatest cause of stress and anxiety, as well as the cause of one being overly concerned. It is fear, as stated, of what might happen in the future.

Of course, we as Christians know that the Lord is the antidote for each of these aspects of fear. Both the Old Testament and the New Testament show us God, who is in complete control of every event. When we are in a right relationship with God, we can be sure that He supervises everything that happens to us. Let us say it in another way:

Whatever happens to a believer is either caused or allowed by God. While the Lord definitely does not cause negative things to happen to us, He does allow such to happen at times. Sometimes it's allowed because of sin within our lives and sometimes because of other things; nevertheless, Satan cannot do anything to a child of God unless he has total permission from the Lord. Even then it's God and not Satan who draws the parameters in totality (Job, Chpts. 1-2).

If we understand this and, thereby, exhibit the proper trust in the Lord, knowing that He does everything for our good, this releases us from all types of fear. To properly love Him is to properly trust Him.

Then again, as we have stated, fear of God is a biblical concept with an intimate link to right relationship with God. To fear God means to acknowledge His power and His authority. To fear God also means to adopt a godly lifestyle out of respect for Him. One who fears God makes those moral choices that reflect the character of the Lord.

## ONLY ONE OPINION IS IMPORTANT

In the New Testament, fear is seen as a source of human motivation. In other words, fear of others' opinions will pressure many to make choices they would not otherwise make. Believers are to remember that only one opinion is important.

Ultimately, we are answerable only to the Lord, thus, we are released by a healthy fear of God from those inferior concerns or even terrors that hold so many of us in their grip.

I had to make that personal decision a long time ago — would I please God, or would I please men. I found out that I couldn't please both. I also knew (and thank the Lord that I did know) that it was God alone who really mattered. While I certainly value the opinion of my fellowman, I do not value it enough to displease God in order to please men.

The New Testament also purifies and further explains the meaning of the fear of the Lord. True fear of God does not include a fear of punishment. Jesus has shown us that God is love. It is love, not dread, that moves us to respond obediently to the Lord.

At the same time, our love for God must always be blended with awe. We must never take God lightly. He is One whose voice shakes the very earth and will soon shatter the heavens (Heb. 12:26-28). The exhortation comes:

*"Let us have grace, whereby we may serve God acceptably with reverence and godly fear: for our God is a consuming fire"* (Heb. 12:28-29).

## THE CROSS

Let us never forget that the consuming fire we worship is also our heavenly Father.

As I close this segment on fear, allow me to repeat myself regarding the believer's proper understanding of the Cross. John said that perfect love casts out fear. So from that we know that love is the great antidote for fear.

Understanding that, the believer can actually only understand the love of God as he ought as he understands the Cross, at least as far as a human being can understand such.

With the proper understanding of such, our faith can then have as its proper object the atonement, which guarantees the help of the Holy Spirit (Rom., Chpt. 8).

This and this alone (I speak of a proper understanding of the Cross and our faith in that finished work) will handle the fear problem. What a blessing that we as Christians have this privilege that the world doesn't have, but how sad that most believers have little understanding of the Cross at all as it concerns their daily living for God.

## POWER

The phrase, *"but of power,"* as given in II Timothy 1:7, could be said, *"the spirit of power,"* for such comes from the Holy Spirit, who definitely occupies the heart and life of the true saint.

Power is definitely needed by the saint of God in every capacity. While we all know the Holy Spirit has this power, in fact, unlimited power, and of every description, the question is, how can we get Him to expend that power on our behalf?

The saint of God is up against the powers of darkness as Paul graphically outlined in Ephesians 6:10-18. To be sure, these powers of darkness are formidable, in fact, so formidable that man in his own personal ingenuity and ability is simply no match. This means that neither humanistic psychology nor anything else that man may conjure up is of any consequence against these powers.

To extend that even further, even the things that are

legitimate in their own right (even all the religious machinations of man), are of little help in this capacity. What do I mean by religious things?

## RELIGIOUS THINGS

For instance, millions of Christians attempt to make the church a defense against these powers of darkness, which definitely come against every true believer. By that I mean that millions think that by the mere fact of belonging to a certain church, that particular association gives them some type of protection. Pure and simple, it doesn't!

While the church, at least if it's a biblical church, is certainly viable in its own right, it serves no purpose whatsoever in this capacity. Others trust in particular manifestations! They think that if some preacher can lay hands on them, and they then experience being slain in the Spirit or another such phenomenon, this is their answer. While some of this is very scriptural and very valid, and it is definitely a blessing and a help to the believer, it will not give the believer victory over the powers of darkness. Now, you should read that very carefully.

Many Christians are led to believe that these manifestations are their answer; consequently, untold thousands of Christians are running all over the world to wherever they think it is that something is happening as it regards these manifestations.

Please don't think I'm minimizing manifestations or the laying on of hands that are truly scriptural. I'm not! I believe in these things, and we practice them in our church constantly because they are biblical.

The wrong is that saints are attempting to use these things for that which was never intended by the Lord. In fact, if these things could give one victory over the world, the flesh, and the Devil, then Jesus came down to this world and died needlessly on a Cross (Gal. 2:21). Others think that the giving of sums of money will merit them something with God. In fact, the list is almost endless.

Almost all of these things we have named are legitimate in their own right, which means they are scriptural, providing they are used correctly. However, as we've already stated, the problem comes when we place our faith in those things and think that by the doing of them, our problem is going to be solved, whatever that problem might be. That is scripturally wrong. Problems will not be solved in that manner!

## DELIVERANCE

Millions of Christians don't even like to hear the word *deliverance* because they automatically think of some terrible bondage of darkness that they don't have, and if they do, they are trying their best to hide it. So, when deliverance is mentioned, it's mentioned only in the sense of an alcoholic, drug addict, etc.

The truth is that millions of Christians (and I think even the majority) actually do have a bondage of some type within their lives. It may not be one of the terrible vices we could name, such as alcohol, immorality, or drugs; however, you would be shocked at the number of Christians who are actually bound by these types of things. Nevertheless, spiritual bondage comes in many shapes, forms, and sizes.

For instance, millions of Christians are bound by gossip. Others are bound by apathy, i.e., lukewarmness (Rev. 3:14-22). In fact, religion is the worst bondage of all!

Most Christians don't think of these things as a bondage, but anything that is contrary to the Word of God and controls the Christian even to some degree can be labeled as none other than a bondage, which means the person needs deliverance.

As stated, it's very hard to get Christians to admit to any type of bondage, much less some of the latter things we have just named. Irrespective, in the eyes of God, these sins are dominating them in some way, and they definitely are sins (Rom. 6:14). In fact, if the spirit of fear of which Paul speaks takes a hold in a person's life, it can be labeled as none other than a bondage, and that person needs deliverance.

One can say without any fear of contradiction that anything in a believer's life that's not *"after the Spirit"* (Rom. 8:1) then, of necessity, must be *"after the flesh"* and is definitely a bondage of some sort.

Now, the question is, how does the Christian get victory over these things?

## EXACTLY WHAT DO WE MEAN BY DELIVERANCE?

People ask us all the time, "Do you have a deliverance ministry?"

Actually, deliverance is the very heart and core of this

ministry! However, when people think of deliverance, they almost always think of it in their own way.

Almost all of the time, in fact, every occasion that comes to my mind, falls into the following category: when individuals ask for deliverance for themselves or someone else, they think of a preacher laying hands on the individual and rebuking the problem (whatever it may be) in the name of Jesus, with the person then being delivered!

In some few cases, that is correct, but mostly, it is wrong! Once again I go back to the statement that if that's all it took to deliver people, then Jesus died needlessly on a cruel Cross.

Let me ask you, the reader, a question: Whenever an individual goes up before a preacher for deliverance, what do you as a Christian think that the Lord is going to do?

Of course, the answer is almost instant — they think that the power of God is going to come upon a person, and the Lord is going to set that person free from whatever the problem is.

As stated, some few times this does happen; however, almost all of the time it doesn't. Why? That's the great question.

To answer that question, we come up with any number of excuses. We say the preacher didn't have the power he should have had, or the favorite expression is that the person seeking help just simply didn't have enough faith. For the most part, none of these things are correct. The answer follows.

## THE CROSS OF CHRIST

The truth is that the Lord is not going to do a single solitary thing to deliver anyone at this particular time for the simple reason that He has already done so. He delivered every single person in this world at the Cross of Calvary. There, every demon was defeated, and Satan's head was bruised exceedingly so (Gen. 3:15). As well, Christ atoned for every sin—past, present, and future—at least for those who will believe, which destroyed Satan's hold on the human race. Satan's legal claim upon humanity is sin, and with sin removed, which Jesus did at the Cross, his legal claim is no more valid.

This is so important, let me say it again: Jesus delivered every single individual at the Cross of Calvary. That means that every person in this world, irrespective of the terrible bondage that may grip them, has, in fact, already been delivered by what Jesus did at the Cross. So, with that being the case, why is it that the world wallows in satanic bondage, with even most Christians living in some type of bondage?

Of course, the answer is very simple. The world will not come to Christ, and for deliverance to be effective, the person must come to Christ. Jesus Himself said, *"And you will not come to Me, that you might have life"* (Jn. 5:40).

What about the millions of Christians who need deliverance as well?

Were not these people delivered when they first came to Christ?

## CHRISTIANS

Every single Christian was delivered of every single sin

when they initially came to Christ. Now, you should read that again and do so carefully, for it is absolutely correct.

Whenever the person was initially saved, no matter when that was, that person was cleansed from all sin, with every single power of darkness totally and completely defeated and broken within that person's life. Paul said that you were washed, sanctified, and justified in the name of the Lord Jesus and by the Spirit of God (I Cor. 6:11).

So, with that being the case, how is it that millions of Christians now live in bondage of one sort or the other?

Whenever the believing sinner (which includes you and me) came to Christ to be saved, we had to simply believe in Christ and believe that He died for us. We didn't have to understand much about it simply because we couldn't understand much about it. However, the Word of God was energized in our hearts by the Holy Spirit, with Him giving us faith to believe, which we did, and at that moment we were saved (Jn. 3:16; Rom. 10:9-10, 13; Eph. 2:8-9; Rev. 22:17).

At that moment, we were literally baptized into the death of Christ, actually buried with Him, and raised with Him in newness of life (Rom. 6:3-5). That means that we were placed *"in Christ,"* which means that all the great victory that He purchased at the Cross with His own precious blood now is our victory simply because it was actually all done on our behalf. Jesus didn't need this, and neither did the holy angels. It was done strictly for us, i.e., for sinners!

That means that when you exhibited faith toward Christ and His sacrifice, in the mind of God, the perfection of Christ, i.e., the righteousness of God, was freely imputed to you. Knowing and understanding that, how is it that Christians can then get off base and get mixed up again in sin, which, of course, causes untold problems?

## THE SIN NATURE

There is a sin nature in all unbelievers. That sin nature (which is a result of the fall) literally controls them and came to them even at birth. It's called "original sin." It refers to what Adam did in the garden of Eden, which has passed down to all men. The moment the believer comes to Christ, the sin nature, although remaining in the Christian, is extinguished so to speak (made to be dormant). In other words, it should not cause the believer any more problems.

What exactly do we mean by a sin nature?

When Adam and Eve sinned, their very nature became that of sin. In other words, everything they did turned out to be sin. Due to the fact that Adam was and is the father of the entirety of the human race so to speak, this means that whatever happened to him would happen to every single person who would be born thereafter. In other words, due to Adam's fall, every single human being that is born is born with a sin nature. It's that something in the unbeliever that propels him totally and completely toward sin. In other words, everything he does in some way, as stated, is sin. It has to be that way because he is spiritually dead (Eph. 2:1-2).

If one is to notice, when the little baby is born, and it

begins to understand things as the months progress, it has to be taught to do right, but it surely doesn't have to be taught to do wrong. It just does those things automatically. That's the sin nature at work, even in those early months of its life, and it only gets worse with time.

Now, some preachers teach that once the person comes to Christ, he has no more sin nature. If that is the case, then why do Christians sin at times? Also, why do some Christians even get to the place that sin controls them, which means that despite all they can do otherwise, they can't stop whatever it is that's controlling them. Let's not pass this off lightly because there are millions of Christians in the shape that I've just mentioned. Are they saved? Yes, they are! They are trusting Christ, and as long as a person is trusting Christ, that person is saved.

## THE STRUGGLE

Now, if they continue in this terrible state that they are in, it's possible that they could lose their souls, even as millions have done down through the centuries, but God doesn't wash us out when we fail. If He did, there wouldn't be any Christians in the world today. Please believe me when I say that there aren't any Christians who have ever lived who haven't had to ask the Lord quite a number of times to forgive them for some particular sins they have committed. The growing process with the child of God is not uneventful, despite what some preachers might claim!

The truth is that with millions of Christians, the sin nature is once again roaring out of control. With many of these people, they are fighting with all of their strength and power to stop whatever it is they are doing, but without success (Rom. 7:15). In fact, the harder they try, the worse the situation becomes, which gets more confusing all the time.

That's the reason that many just simply quit. They've done all they know to do, and they've done all they have been told to do by particular preachers, but it has all been to no avail. The bondage, whatever it might be, is not better, but worse.

Now, what are we to do with these people? Well, we can excommunicate them or punish them — or whatever. However, I would quickly remind the reader that most of the time, those who are screaming the loudest for the severest punishment are probably in worse shape spiritually speaking than the ones they are attempting to punish. No, that's not the answer.

## HOW IS IT THAT A CHRISTIAN DRIFTS BACK INTO THIS DILEMMA OF SIN?

As we've already stated, the moment any believing sinner comes to Christ, he is delivered from every bondage of darkness and cleansed from every sin.

So, how is it that he can once again become embroiled in sin to where he is in bondage?

When you as a believing sinner gave your heart to Christ, you were so happy and thrilled, and you felt that you would never sin again. To be sure, every true believer hates sin.

But then, you found out that very shortly, you failed the Lord. It scared you, and you resolved in your mind and spirit never to do that again, whatever it was. And so, to keep from doing it again, you placed your faith in something other than the Cross of Christ. It really doesn't matter what it was; if it wasn't the Cross, it was going to cause you problems. That's when the sin nature revived.

Most of the time, instead of going to the Cross, we get deeper involved in works of the flesh because that's what it really is. Then we find that the sin nature is once again beginning to operate within our lives. We find some problems in our lives getting worse and worse, and we really are a little bit confused, not understanding. We believe that Jesus Christ has set us free, and we will confess to being free, but, in truth, we aren't.

As we have stated, when the person comes to Christ, the sin nature is made dormant. While it remains in the heart and life of the believer, it is unplugged so to speak and will cause no trouble. The problem comes in with our faith placed in the wrong object, and every time that happens, the sin nature revives and begins to cause us great problems. I'm going to make a statement that some of you may doubt, but I know it's true.

Ninety-nine percent of all believers in the world are controlled by the sin nature and are living in a state of bondage of some sort. How do I know that?

I know it simply because the modern church doesn't understand the solution to this problem — the answer to this dilemma — not at all. That solution is the Cross of Christ.

While most every believer understands the Cross as it regards salvation, as it pertains to sanctification, they simply don't have a clue. So that means, if the truth be told, that the modern church simply doesn't know how to live for God. That doesn't mean they aren't saved and they aren't Spirit-filled, and it doesn't mean that they don't love the Lord. They do! In reality, they are trying with all of their strength, but they are trying in the wrong way.

So, that's the way the sin nature once again comes alive in our hearts and lives and ultimately begins to control us, which makes life miserable to say the least. That's what Paul was talking about when he said:

*"For that which I do I allow not* (should have been translated 'I understand not'): *for what I would, that do I not* (what I want to do, which is to live righteously and holy, I find I cannot); *but what I hate, that do I* (refers to doing the very thing he doesn't want to do. Some would say that if that's the case, then he's not responsible. Oh, yes, he is, as all of us are responsible for failure)" (Rom. 7:15).

While Paul was responsible, and while we are responsible, as well, it's not responsibility as we think of such.

### JUST SAY NO!

Most Christians are taught to just simply say no to sin. The first thing we must understand is that sin is so powerful that a simple no will not do the trick so to speak. We are speaking of the most powerful factor in the universe other than the power of God. Please believe me when I say that there is no simple solution to it other than the Cross.

Coming up in a particular Pentecostal denomination, I heard preachers say time and time again, "All they had to do was say no and walk away." Then they would quickly add, "And because they didn't do that, that shows that they were not sincere to begin with." And then they would quickly add, "We are better off without them."

It's not that simple!

Sin is propelled by the powers of darkness, and those powers are lethal. They are more powerful than you and I ever thought of being. So, we have only one way of defeating this power of darkness. Please read this statement again as given by Paul after he had learned God's prescribed order of victory:

*"For the law of the Spirit of life in Christ Jesus has made me free from the law of sin and death"* (Rom. 8:2).

The law of sin and death is the most powerful law in the world other than the law of the Spirit of life in Christ Jesus. The short phrase, *"in Christ Jesus,"* refers to what He did at the Cross of Calvary. Now that the believer is in bondage to sin in some nature and in some way, how does he get out of this dilemma?

## THE CROSS OF CHRIST IS THE ONLY ANSWER

Let me say it again: The Cross of Christ is the only answer to this dilemma, which means that it's not one of several. Unfortunately, the church has held up psychology as the answer, which is an insult to what Christ did at the Cross and in His resurrection. Now let's see how the Cross is the answer.

Paul said that the Holy Spirit would give us power, which is the word of our present study.

We all know that the Holy Spirit is God and, as such, has unlimited power. The question is, how do I get Him to exert this power on my behalf?

There's only one way that He will do that, and it is according to the following:

The work of Christ on the Cross on behalf of lost sinners was and is a legal work. In fact, before the Cross, the Holy Spirit could not even come and dwell in the hearts and lives of believers, with the exception of short periods of time with particular prophets, etc. In other words, He could not make His abode in their hearts and lives. In fact, one of the last words that Jesus related to His disciples concerned this of which we speak. He said, *"For He* (the Holy Spirit) *dwells with you* (even as He did all Old Testament saints)*, and shall be in you* (that which would take place after the Cross and after the day of Pentecost)*"* (Jn. 14:17).

We are trying to say that every single thing the Holy Spirit did was predicated on the Cross of Christ. What Jesus did at the Cross constitutes the legal parameters in which the Holy Spirit works, and works exclusively. In other words, He will not go outside of those parameters. That's how important the Cross actually is.

Now, if, in fact, it is that important (and to be sure, it definitely is), then it makes sense that we understand all that we can about the Cross. Every believer should make it his life's work to understand the Cross and to learn about the Cross. He should ask the Holy Spirit to show him about the Cross, which He most definitely will do. However, the Holy Spirit doesn't require us to be scholars in order to obtain the great benefits of the Cross. He only demands one thing, and that one thing is faith! What do we mean by that?

## THE OBJECT OF YOUR FAITH

We mean that the object of your faith must be that through which the Holy Spirit works, which is the Cross of Christ. You must place your faith there totally and completely and understand that every blessing that you receive comes through what Jesus did at Calvary. Every blessing means every good thing from God, and that is from salvation to the ultimate — the coming glorification at the resurrection. All and without exception come through what Jesus did at the Cross.

Placing your faith in that great finished work, and maintaining it in that great finished work, means that you're not placing it in yourself, in a church denomination, in particular preachers, or anything else for that matter — only the Cross. When this is done, the Holy Spirit will then begin to work on your behalf simply because you are now functioning in the great work that Jesus has done on your behalf. He will then expend His great power for you, through you, and within you, and in every manner, giving you victory on all counts (Rom. 8:2). That and that alone is the way and means by which the power of the Holy Spirit is expended on your behalf on a continuing basis.

## SPIRIT-FILLED CHRISTIANS

Many Spirit-filled Christians think that the very fact of one being Spirit-filled guarantees a constant flow of Holy Spirit power (Acts 1:8). It doesn't! The potential is there but only if we function as we should. In fact, if this Holy Spirit power was constant, don't you think that there would never be a single failure of any kind among Spirit-filled Christians. As well, all such Christians would be totally and completely mature in the Lord.

Now, we all know that the above is not the case at all. So, what is wrong?

When Jesus said, *"But you shall receive power, after that the Holy Spirit is come upon you,"* did He not mean what He said (Acts 1:8)? Most definitely He did, and most definitely He does! To be sure, this is power that can overcome anything. As well, it is totally and completely at our disposal. So why isn't this power working in the hearts and lives of all Spirit-filled believers?

The truth is that anyone who is Spirit-filled does have the Holy Spirit working within his life to some measure. With many, it's not much, but it's at least some. However, this of which Jesus actually spoke (I speak of the effectual working of this mighty power within our lives on a continuing basis) can only come about in one manner.

As we have repeatedly stated, we are to place our faith exclusively in the Cross of Christ. We are then to believe that the Holy Spirit is going to do for us what needs to be done, and to be sure, He definitely shall. That is the only way that the full power of the Holy Spirit can be manifested within the believer's life. The Spirit will not deviate from that, will not veer from that, and will not function in any other capacity (Rom. 8:1-2).

## THE LINKING OF THE HOLY SPIRIT AND THE CROSS

Most Christians have little idea of how important the Cross is as it regards the Holy Spirit.

The Old Testament always furnishes for us a firm foundation of all that we have in the New Testament. When we go back to the Old, we find that it is the Holy Spirit who actually resided in the Holy of Holies of the tabernacle and the temple. In fact, every single thing done by the Godhead on this earth (other than the sacrifice of Christ) is always and without exception done by the person, power, office, and ministry of the Holy Spirit.

In Old Testament times, it was a physical building that was the house of the Holy Spirit so to speak, whereas now, due to what Christ has done at the Cross, the believer is actually the house or temple of the Holy Spirit (I Cor. 3:16). Of course, in some sense, actually, in essence, the entirety of the Godhead is in every member of the Godhead.

To show you the importance of the Cross, even in Old

Testament times, when the high priest went into the Holy of Holies once a year, which was on the Great Day of Atonement, he could not go in without blood. He had to kill a bullock (Lev., Chpt. 16) and take the blood of that animal into the Holy of Holies and apply it to the mercy seat that rested on the ark of the covenant between the two cherubim. Of course, the blood of the slain animal represented the shed blood of the One who was to come, the Lord Jesus Christ. If the high priest had gone in without that blood, he would have been stricken dead immediately.

## THE ALTAR

Likewise, whenever any priest went into the Holy Place, which was immediately in front of the Holy of Holies and was separated only by a veil, he took a censer. In that censer he had to have coals of fire over which was poured incense. The coals of fire had to be taken from the brazen altar.

Of course, the altar represented the Cross of Christ, with the fire representing the judgment of God that came upon God's Son instead of us. The coals of fire had to come from that altar, and if they didn't come from that altar, the priests would be killed, even as were Nadab and Abihu, sons of Aaron, who *"offered strange fire before the LORD"* (Lev. 10:1-3).

In fact, when those two died, fire came out from the Holy of Holies (actually, from the Holy Spirit), passed through the veil without burning it, and struck these two men, killing them on the spot. In essence, the Holy Spirit was saying, "Everything must be done through the Cross and by the Cross, and if not, death will be the result!"

## JUDGMENT AND THE CROSS

Some may erroneously think that the day of grace in which we now live cancels out all of that of which we have just spoken. To be frank, it is the opposite way around.

Paul said, *"And the times of this ignorance* (Old Testament times) *God winked at* (meaning that judgment was expended only on a few)*; but now* (this day of grace) *commands all men everywhere to repent"* (Acts 17:30).

I maintain that the judgment of God is now coming upon believers to a far greater extent than it did in Old Testament times.

Before the Cross, the Gentile world was completely ignorant of the things of God. Consequently, except in a few cases, judgment was withheld, at least as far as this life is concerned. It was the same with Israel.

The Lord at times exacted judgment upon His people, but not nearly to the extent that they deserved because they were attempting to function from the respect of the shadow instead of the substance. In other words, the Cross was not then a fact, only a distant promise.

Due to the fact of the Cross and the dissemination of the gospel all over the world, which is the Message of the Cross, that is, if it's the true message, God expects far more presently than He did in the days before the Cross. Everything is tied to the Cross, as everything must be tied to the Cross.

## THE LORD'S SUPPER

To show you how serious all of this is, Paul said when speaking of the Lord's Supper:

*"Wherefore whosoever shall eat this bread, and drink this cup of the Lord, unworthily, shall be guilty of the body and blood of the Lord.*

*"But let a man examine himself, and so let him eat of that bread, and drink of that cup."*

He then said, *"For he who eats and drinks unworthily, eats and drinks damnation to himself, not discerning the Lord's body.*

*"For this cause many are weak and sickly among you, and many sleep* (die before their time)*"* (I Cor. 11:27-30).

What did Paul mean by eating and drinking unworthily?

He was speaking of not properly discerning the Lord's body.

The entirety of the Lord's Supper speaks of the death of Christ on the Cross — Him giving Himself in sacrifice in order that we might be saved. As should be obvious, the broken bread speaks of His body that was pierced and broken, in a sense, on the Cross. The cup, of course, speaks of His shed blood.

He said, *"As oft as you do this,"* the taking of these emblems, *"do ye … In remembrance of Me"* (I Cor. 11:24-25).

Furthermore, He said this should be done *"till He come"* (I Cor. 11:26).

By all of this, He is simply meaning that we are to understand as believers that we have salvation strictly and completely because of what He did at the Cross on our behalf. We are to understand, as well, that everything else comes from the Cross to us, such as healing, victory, overcoming strength, communion with the Lord, and power, in other words, everything!

If we fail to understand this, we are not properly discerning the Lord's body, and when we take the Lord's Supper, it can cause us great problems, as should be obvious.

## THE CROSS OF CHRIST

I firmly believe that this is the reason that many Christians are sick and that many die prematurely. While they don't lose their souls, they do lose much in this life. Actually, that's what Paul said when he used the word *many.*

I'm trying to say to the reader that the atonement, i.e., the Cross of Christ, is not to be tampered with.

All unbelievers in this world will die eternally lost if they do not trust Christ and what He did at the Cross as it regards their salvation. Likewise, while not losing their souls, all believers will definitely suffer defeat in almost every capacity if they don't understand that all blessings and all victory come totally and completely through and by the Cross of Christ and our faith in the Cross. As the sinner cannot have salvation without faith in Christ and the Cross, likewise, the believer cannot have victory outside of the Cross.

There could be nothing more important for you as a

believer than to have a proper understanding of the Cross and to place your faith exclusively in that finished work. Everything, and I mean everything, hinges on that.

## THE CONDITION OF THE MODERN CHURCH RELATIVE TO THE CROSS

In the 1950s, certain parts of the church began to embrace humanistic psychology as the answer to man's dilemma. Regrettably, in the 1960s, some Pentecostal denominations began to go in the same direction. In the 1980s, most Full Gospel denominations embraced this false philosophy altogether. At the present time, the general headquarters of the Assemblies of God in Springfield, Missouri, and the Church of God, with headquarters in Cleveland, Tennessee, recommend strongly the twelve-step programs of the psychological way. In other words, this is their answer to the ills of man, which is the same answer as the atheists would give.

Regrettably, most of the laity do not know, realize, or understand the acute danger in all of this as it regards spiritual things.

The Word of God claims to have all the answers as it regards man's condition. That answer is Jesus Christ and Him crucified. The psychological way is something else altogether, as would be obvious. Consequently, it's not possible to have both!

So, for all practical purposes, the modern church has totally abandoned the Cross of Christ in favor of the rudiments of this present world. They have either done so through scriptural ignorance or rank unbelief. Nevertheless, that is the direction that the majority of the church world has gone.

## DENYING THE CROSS

Thankfully, there are some voices here and there, mostly in the evangelical world, that have been raised up against this evil of psychology, and evil it is! Regrettably, there are precious few voices who are Pentecostal (other than my own), who are raising any objections whatsoever. In fact, I'm not aware of any other Pentecostals who are raising objections. The shame of all shames is that people who call themselves Spirit-filled would rather opt for a humanistic way that is totally opposite of the Word of God.

So, that's the condition of the modern church world presently. It has abandoned the Cross, if not altogether denying the Cross. Consequently, it can only be said that it has a form of godliness but denies the power thereof. The Scripture plainly and unequivocally says *"from such turn away"* (II Tim. 3:5).

As previously stated, in 1997, the Lord began to open up to me the revelation of the Cross. To be sure, even as someone has well said, "Desperation precedes revelation." This was certainly the situation in my case. In desperation I cried to the Lord, and in that desperation, the Lord graciously and wondrously answered. To be sure, it didn't come quickly or easily, but thankfully, it did come. The Lord told me the following:

- The answer for which you seek is found only in the Cross (Rom. 6:3-5, 11, 14; Gal. 6:14).
- You are to place your faith exclusively in the Cross of Christ, i.e., the finished work (I Cor. 1:17-18; 2:2).
- When you place your faith exclusively in the finished work of Christ, the Holy Spirit will then do great and mighty things on your behalf (Rom. 8:1-11; Col. 2:10-15).

Of course, I have greatly oversimplified a very complex explanation. However, if you the reader will begin with what I've said, even as the Lord started me along the same path, the Spirit of God will greatly begin to enlarge to you all the great rudiments of the Cross of Christ. In fact, it will never end because the potential of the Cross is inexhaustible.

## THE DIVIDING LINE

The Cross of Christ is the dividing line between the true church and the apostate church. In fact, it has always been that way, actually beginning with Cain and Abel (Gen., Chpt. 4).

All of this means that people and preachers who ignore the Cross, demean the Cross, or make it less than it is are going to go into spiritual oblivion. It is only those who understand the veracity of the Cross and what it all means according to the Word of God who *"shall be strong, and do exploits"* (Dan. 11:32).

Those who look to the Cross are looking to that which God has provided, and at great price to Himself I might quickly add.

Those who place their faith in something else, irrespective as to what the something else is, in essence, are saying that they want something other than the Cross.

The Cross of Christ exposes the flesh, and that is where the rub comes. Paul referred to it as *"the offence of the Cross"* (Gal. 5:11). Whenever people are told (especially preachers) that all of the things they have been doing are, in effect, of no consequence, it doesn't sit too well. In other words, it is an offense. It was very hard for the Jews of Paul's day to abandon the law of Moses. It was their identity. They had functioned according to this law (at least to some degree) for the last nearly 1,600 years. Now this upstart apostle was telling them that he had had a vision of the Lord, and he had been given the meaning of the new covenant, and that meaning was the Cross. That meant that the ceremonial and the ritualistic law was no more. Jesus Christ had settled the issue by fulfilling all the demands of the law, so there was no more purpose in having the shadow when the substance was available.

## AND OF LOVE

The three word phrase, *"and of love,"* comes from II Tim. 1:7. It presents the spirit of love as again given by the Holy Spirit.

Whenever the believing sinner comes to Christ, the divine nature comes into the believer's heart as well. With that comes divine love, the God kind of love. The Greek word is *agape.*

The world doesn't have this type of love, cannot have this type of love, and, in fact, will not have this type of love unless they come to Christ. In fact, love is one of the fruits of the Spirit (Gal. 5:22).

However, this love cannot be developed in the heart and life of the believer, even as fruit must be developed, unless the believer has a proper understanding of the Cross of Christ, not only as it relates to salvation, but as it relates to sanctification.

As we've already stated, the Cross was and is the greatest example of love that humanity has ever known and will ever know. In fact, the fruit of the Spirit as a whole cannot be developed in the life of the believer unless he understands that it is through the Cross that all of these great things come to us. Now, let's look at that a moment.

I dare say that most believers would have little understanding as it regards the fruit of the Spirit coming to us through the Cross; however, the Cross of Christ is the only means and the only way by which God can give anything to anyone. We may erroneously think it's our great faith that gets us all of these things; however, while faith definitely plays a part, and a great part at that, it's really the object of faith that makes all the difference. In other words, for faith to be faith, at least that which God will recognize and honor, it must be faith in the Cross.

As should be understood, all of these great things done for the believer come through the person and office of the Holy Spirit. He is the One who carries out all work in our hearts and lives. However, as we've already explained, He does so exclusively as it regards our faith in the finished work of Christ. If the reader gets tired of reading about this, so be it. I want to say it and say it in so many ways that no one will have any doubt as to what I'm saying. I do this, first of all, because I believe the Lord would have me do so, and secondly, because I know and realize that Satan hinders greatly the truth of the Word, so it has to be given over and over.

## THE MANNER OF SATAN'S DECEPTIONS

I want you to look at the following very closely, and I think it will help you to understand some things:

First of all, Satan greatly opposes truth, while he opposes lies or half-truths not at all. The parable of the sower aptly brings this out.

Jesus said, *"Hear ye therefore the parable of the sower. When anyone hears the Word of the kingdom, and understands it not, then comes the wicked one, and catches away that which was sown in his heart"* (Mat. 13:18-19).

That's the reason it's so hard to learn these truths that we are attempting to bring to you. It is simply because they are the Word of God, and Satan does everything he can do to hinder you from understanding what is being said.

With all error comes some truth, which deceives the hearers. In other words, they hear the truth and accept the truth, but at the same time, they are accepting error placed in the truth. Jesus dealt with this, as well:

*"Another parable spoke He unto them; The kingdom of heaven is like unto leaven* (error), *which a woman took, and hid in three measures of meal* (in the Word of God), *till the whole was leavened"* (Mat. 13:33).

As is obvious, the Word of God is righteous and pure; however, if someone mixes error with it, which is done constantly, the error (leaven) will ultimately take over the whole. In other words, one of Satan's favorite tactics is to get preachers to preach some truth, which is acceptable, and then to insert some error. The truth becomes the bait in order that the error might be presented.

Error always appeals to baser motives in one's heart and life. In other words, the "greed gospel," as I refer to such, appeals to greed, of which all of us seem to have some. Error can appeal to lust, can appeal to the desire for place and position, for recognition, etc. In other words, as stated, there is something in the heart of a person that's not right that leans toward self-will, etc., in which the error finds lodging and is, therefore, accepted.

As well, all deception has a spirit behind it that is powerful and strong, which plays on these things I've mentioned. To be frank, it takes the power of God to break one out of deception, and to be sure, religion is the greatest deception of all, actually being a narcotic one might say.

The true love of God will always accept the Cross, as should be understandable. If the Cross is rejected, power is then rejected as well as love, and now we come to the third part.

## AND OF A SOUND MIND

This short phrase carries the same connotation as the others — *"the spirit of a sound mind."* The scholars say that a *"spirit of self-control"* would be better rendered.

Self-control has to do with the will, and inasmuch as this is so very important, it will be good for us to address ourselves to this again.

Most Christians have the erroneous idea that on becoming a believer, the will is made super strong; consequently, all one has to do to avoid sin is just simply say no! If they don't do such a thing, then they think that means they want to do whatever it is they are being tempted to do.

While that certainly may be true of some few cases as it regards believers, it's not correct at all regarding most.

Most Christians do not want to fail the Lord and, in fact, are fighting with all their strength not to fail the Lord. The idea of some type of super will is totally wrong and has no scriptural backing whatsoever. In fact, if the will is all that the Christian uses in order to overcome sin, that particular Christian is going to fail the Lord, and of that there is no doubt.

Paul said as much in Romans 7:18:

*"For to will is present with me; but how to perform that which is good I find not."*

He wants to obey God, and, in fact, the will is present for him to do that, but these passions, whatever they might be, are stronger than the will, so he fails.

## PAUL

Some may argue that all of this happened with Paul before his conversion; however, that is totally in error. Even a cursory study of Romans, Chapter 7, disproves a before-conversion experience.

These things happened to Paul not long after he got saved and was baptized with the Holy Spirit as recorded in Acts, Chapter 9. At that time he didn't know God's prescribed order of victory through the Cross, so he was living a life of spiritual failure, even as all do so who go that route, which sadly incorporates almost all of the modern church.

When it comes to the will of the believer, he has one of two choices as it regards this all-important factor in his life. He can *will* to go God's way, which is the Cross, or he can *will* to do otherwise. That's as far as the will can go.

If he chooses to do otherwise, he will find his will overcome despite all of his efforts to not do what Satan is tempting him to do. The simple truth is that the will is no match for Satan or his spirits of darkness.

If the believer chooses to go God's way of the Cross, then he definitely will have the willpower to say yes to Christ in every capacity.

## WHAT IS THE WAY OF THE LORD?

The way of the Lord, which is the way of victory in every capacity, is the way of the Cross.

That means the following:

First of all, let's deal with the unsaved: It doesn't matter how far gone the sinner might be, or how bound in sin he might be (even in the last stages of alcoholism or drug addiction);

if the sinner desires to do so, he can say yes to the Lord Jesus Christ. He might not be able to say no to alcohol or a hundred and one other vices, but God protects his will to the extent that he can say yes to Christ if he chooses to do so.

If he says yes to Christ, then the Lord can get him out of alcoholism or any other problem he might have. The answer for this man or woman is not in saying no to these vices, which, in fact, he is unable to do. His answer is in saying yes to Christ.

When it comes to Christians, it works on the same principle. The believer, no matter how weak he is, has the capacity to say yes to Christ. When I speak of saying yes to Christ, I'm actually referring to saying yes to the Cross. That and that alone is the answer (I Cor. 1:17-18; 2:2; Gal. 6:14; Col. 2:10-15).

Inasmuch as the Cross is the answer to all things, it is to that great work to which we must say yes. Of course, we're referring to what Jesus there did, which includes His resurrection and even His exaltation.

When you the believer say yes to the Cross of Christ, which you have the willpower to do, and which God guarantees, victory is then yours.

Paul said:

*"Likewise reckon* (say yes) *you also yourselves to be dead indeed unto sin, but alive unto God through Jesus Christ our Lord"* (Rom. 6:11).

However, one can do this that Paul says only because one has placed his faith in the finished work of Christ exactly as the apostle has been describing in the previous verses.

When one says yes to the Cross, one does not have to bother about saying no to the devil. The one admonition covers it all.

## DEAD TO SIN

In fact, why should we have any conversation at all with that to which we are dead? Paul plainly said, *"Reckon you also yourselves to be dead indeed unto sin."* With that being the case, we should have no conversation with it whatsoever.

If we are *"alive unto God through Jesus Christ our Lord,"* our conversation should be to Him and to Him only.

Many Christians speak about saying no to sin or the Devil when such is completely unnecessary. I am no longer alive to that world of sin, Satan, evil spirits, etc. I'm not trying to overcome those types of things simply because Jesus has already overcome those things for me. He did so at the Cross and in His resurrection. Consequently, instead of saying no to sin, to which I am dead, I will simply say yes to Christ.

The moment you start saying no, or anything for that matter, to sin, to Satan, to the powers of darkness, or even to temptation, you are in some way admitting that the thing is alive and well within your life. With that not being the case, why have any conversation with it whatsoever?

## YES AND AMEN

Since the Lord showed me the great victory of the Cross, I

haven't had to say no to anything the Devil has from then until now. Such never crosses my mind. Does Satan ever tempt?

Yes, he does! However, I overcome him by simply saying yes to Christ. Let's remember what Paul said:

*"For all the promises of God in Him* (in Christ) *are yea* (yes)*, and in Him Amen* (meaning it is truth, and it will not change)*, unto the glory of God by us"* (II Cor. 1:20).

What does Paul mean by every promise being yes?

He is meaning that God will not change His mind about what Jesus has done at the Cross. Every single victory afforded us by the great sacrifice of the Cross will never change. Notice, the apostle said *"in Him,"* meaning Christ. We must always remember that when we say *"in Him"* or *"in Christ,"* we're not merely referring to Christ per se, but rather what He did at the Cross.

If I remember correctly, Paul used the term *"in Christ"* or one of its derivatives, such as *"in Him,"* about 170 times. Every single time he used the phrase, he was speaking of what Christ did at the Cross.

So, when the apostle spoke of a *"sound mind"* or *"self-control,"* he was speaking of that which is given by the Holy Spirit to all believers. Please allow me one more thought: If you will understand that all your victory comes through the Cross of Christ and keep yourself in that capacity, you will find your mental capacities becoming sharper and sharper. The reason is simple:

*"Let this mind be in you, which was also in Christ Jesus."*

In regard to this he said, *"He humbled Himself, and*

*became obedient unto death, even the death of the Cross"* (Phil. 2:5, 8).

## THE GARMENT OF PRAISE

What I am about to say, I have already said twice in this volume, that is, if I remember correctly. However, it is so important that I want to make sure that you understand it and appropriate it unto yourself, which will help change your life. The great prophet Isaiah said, *"To give unto them ... The garment of praise for the spirit of heaviness"* (Isa. 61:3).

I won't go into great detail, actually already having done that. It is just to stir your pure mind by way of remembrance. In your waking hours, the moment your mind dwells on the Lord, start praising the Lord. You don't have to do it out loud, actually, under your breath, even in your spirit will be sufficient. Just start thanking Him for what He has done for you, for who He is, for what He means to you, etc. In just a few moments' time, your mind will wander to something else, but in a little bit, it will again dwell on the Lord. Again, you are to begin to praise Him, and do so until your mind shifts to something else. You are to do this every waking moment that you think about the Lord or His work.

This I promise: When you set about to do this, you will find that fear must leave. You will find that discouragement and depression must go. You will find temptation will have no place anymore. The spirit of heaviness will leave because you are filling your mind and spirit with the presence of the Lord.

Please remember that these praises are not for the Lord; they really are for you. So, if you want to get rid of fear, oppression, and discouragement, do what I have said and keep it up, and you will find the victory promised by the Cross.

I realize the world does not understand at all, and neither does most of the church, exactly how a proper faith in the Cross of Christ will improve the mentality of an individual; however, it definitely will! In fact, it will not only improve one mentally but physically, domestically, intellectually, and above all, spiritually. In fact, the Cross of Christ is the throughway to all blessings. Your praising the Lord as we have mentioned, and in the way that we have mentioned, is all made possible by the Cross of Christ.

## SIN AND THE CROSS

We do not properly understand sin until we first of all understand the Cross. When I speak of understanding the Cross, I am speaking of understanding it relative not only to salvation, which most believers do understand, but, as well, our sanctification. This pertains to how we live for God on a daily basis, how we have victory over the world, the flesh, and the Devil, and how we grow in grace and the knowledge of the Lord.

It was at the Cross that all sin was addressed and properly atoned, and to be sure, it was our sins that put Him there. Once one sees the Cross and sees it properly (I'm referring to the Cross as it applies to our everyday life and living), then one begins to see sin in its proper light. It's not a pretty picture.

The reason that one can then see and understand sin to a greater degree is because now (since understanding the Cross) one properly sees oneself. Again, the picture is not pleasant to behold!

The Cross of Christ shows everything up for what it actually is. It tells us how black sin is and how ungodly we are, and none of us enjoy very much hearing such a truth.

When one properly sees the Cross, one then properly sees his own unrighteousness. He begins to see and understand that his only hope is in Christ and what Christ did at the Cross. He ceases to look to his own righteousness, realizing how far short it falls. Once again, all of this comes about because of a proper understanding of the Cross. Regrettably, not many in the modern church understand the Cross, at least as it refers to our sanctification. Quite possibly, they do not desire to understand it, and that is for all the obvious reasons.

The Cross of Christ exposes man for what he really is — totally unable to save himself in any capacity — and cries for who He really is — the Saviour of mankind. Man is not too happy about admitting to either.

## WHY IS THE CROSS SO IMPORTANT?

The Cross alone deals with sin. Nothing else will as nothing else can. This is the reason the Cross of Christ is so important, actually, the single most important thing that mankind faces. Without the Cross, there is no remission of sin. When we use the term "the Cross," we are actually speaking of what Jesus did there in the giving of Himself in the shedding of His own precious blood (Eph. 2:13-18). That's the reason the church sins so greatly when it ignores the Cross and, thereby, substitutes its own so-called remedy. It is the story of Cain all over again.

We've said it repeatedly, and we'll say it again: The only thing standing between mankind and eternal hell is the Cross of Christ. The only thing standing between the church and apostasy is the Cross of Christ.

## ERRONEOUS DIRECTIONS

There are many who think that we are harsh and, thereby, criticize us greatly because we point out the terrible error of *The Purpose Driven Life* debacle. We do so because, as stated, it's the sin of Cain all over again. It is the substitute of something other than the Cross of Christ. The same can be said for the Word of Faith doctrine, plus denominationalism, etc. This is the reason that humanistic psychology is so wrong. All of these efforts are an attempt to deal with sin by means other than the Cross.

Let me say it again: There is only one remedy for sin, and that is the Cross of Christ.

Paul said:

*"But this Man* (this Priest, Christ Jesus), *after He had offered one sacrifice for sins forever* (speaks of the Cross), *sat down on the right hand of God* (refers to the great contrast

with the priests under the Levitical system, who never sat down because their work was never completed; the work of Christ was a 'finished work' and needed no repetition);

*"From henceforth expecting till His enemies be made His footstool.* (These enemies are Satan and all the fallen angels and demon spirits, plus all who follow Satan.)

*"For by one offering He has perfected forever them who are sanctified.* (Everything one needs is found in the Cross [Gal. 6:14])" (Heb. 10:12-14).

## WILLFUL SIN AND UNWILLFUL SIN

No sin is excusable before God or man, irrespective of if it's willful or unwillful. In some way it will still bring about its catastrophic results. We must never forget that.

What is the difference in willful sin and unwillful sin?

Willful sin is that sin indulged and engaged by, for example, Achan and his family. Inward, as stated, there seems to be little temptation. While temptation for the Christian is in some ways always present, still, temptation was really not Achan's problem, but rather self-will (Josh. 7:18-21).

For instance, as we bring it up to modern times, when believers purposefully set a course that is wrong simply because that is what they want to do (which has been the case untold millions of times down through the ages), that is willful sin. At the present time, there are hundreds, if not thousands, of religious leaders who know better but simply because they desire to curry the favor of others, they embark upon a course that is not of God, meaning that it is not scriptural. It might be popular and, in fact, almost everything that Satan has in the religious sense is popular, but, of course, it is not scriptural; therefore, it is wrong, dead wrong!

## WRONG DIRECTION

One might say that every single preacher who follows *The Purpose Driven Life* scheme is engaging in willful sin. They know better, and if they don't know better, they certainly ought to know better if they call themselves preachers.

All willful sin in some way starts with a rejection of the Cross of Christ. In other words, the individual makes a conscious decision that he, for whatever reason or reasons, will not accept the Cross as the answer to man's dilemma, but rather chooses something else. That is willful sin. It is the sin of Judas.

Can one repent of such a sin? He most definitely can, and the Lord will most definitely forgive, cleanse, wash, and restore (I Jn. 1:9); however, the truth is, most will not repent, but rather plunge deeper into the morass of wrong direction. Listen to Paul:

"*Beware of dogs* (the apostle is addressing the Judaizers, who were Jews from Jerusalem who claimed Christ but insisted on believer's keeping the law as well; all of this was diametrically opposed to Paul's gospel of grace, in which the law of Moses had no part; as well, by the use of the word *dogs*, the apostle was using the worst slur. In fact, the word *dogs* was used by Jews for homosexuals; so, Paul is, in essence, saying that these Judaizers were to the gospel of Jesus Christ as homosexuality is to the human race — a perversion of the worst order.), *beware of evil workers* (they denigrated the Cross), *beware of the concision.* (This presents a Greek word Paul uses as a play upon the Greek word *circumcision,* which was at the heart of the law gospel of the Judaizers)" (Phil. 3:2).

## ENEMIES OF THE CROSS OF CHRIST

The apostle then said, *"Brethren, be followers together of me* (be fellow-imitators)*, and mark them which walk so as you have us for an ensample* (observe intently).

*"(For many walk* (speaks of those attempting to live for God outside of the victory and rudiments of the Cross of Christ)*, of whom I have told you often, and now tell you even weeping* (this is a most serious matter)*, that they are the enemies of the Cross of Christ* (those who do not look exclusively to the Cross of Christ must be labeled 'enemies')*:

*"Whose end is destruction* (if the Cross is denied or ignored, the loss of the soul is the only ultimate conclusion)*, whose god is their belly* (refers to those who attempt to pervert the gospel for their own personal gain)*, and whose glory is in their shame* (the material things they seek, God labels as 'shame')*, who mind earthly things.)* (This means they have no interest in heavenly things, which signifies they are using the Lord for their own personal gain)" (Phil. 3:17-19).

## UNWILLFUL SIN

Such sin (unwillful sin) concerns sin in which the believer engages but doesn't want to do so and, in fact, is trying with all his might and strength not to do so, but fails anyway. Chapter 7 of Romans is replete with this information.

When Paul wrote Chapter 7, he was writing it about himself; however, the information given pertained to the time immediately after his conversion and baptism with the Holy Spirit, but yet, with a lack of knowledge as it regarded how to live for God. For a period of time, possibly even several years, he tried to live for God by the keeping of commandments, regrettably and sadly, almost identically to the manner in which most of the modern church functions.

When he wrote Chapter 7, he understood perfectly the ways of the Lord as it regarded victory because the Lord had already given him the revelation as it regarded the meaning of the new covenant, which, in effect, was and is the meaning of the Cross.

However, the apostle was inspired by the Holy Spirit to tell us that unless we follow the prescribed order laid down by the Lord, which is found in Chapter 6 of Romans, we will repeat Chapter 7 of Romans all over again, no matter how hard we may try to function otherwise. In other words, the sin nature, which results in the law of sin and death, is ruling in such a believer's life. Let me say it again: Regrettably, due to modern believers having such little knowledge of the Cross, at least as it refers to sanctification, the sin nature is ruling most Christians.

Perhaps Chapter 7 of Romans can be summed up in Verse 15.

## THE WORD OF THE LORD

The apostle said:

"*For that which I do* (the failure) *I allow not* (should have been translated, 'I understand not'; these are not the words of an unsaved man as some claim, but rather a believer who is trying and failing): *for what I would, that do I not* (refers to the obedience he wants to render to Christ, but rather fails; why? as Paul explained, the believer is married to Christ but is being unfaithful to Christ by spiritually cohabiting with the law, which frustrates the grace of God; that means the Holy Spirit will not help such a person, which guarantees failure [Gal. 2:21]); *but what I hate, that do I* (refers to sin in his life, which he doesn't want to do and, in fact, hates, but finds himself unable to stop; unfortunately, due to the fact of not understanding the Cross as it refers to sanctification, this is, as stated, the plight of most modern Christians)" (Rom. 7:15).

Now, don't misunderstand, even though such a believer (even as Paul) is trying hard not to fail the Lord and, in fact, hates the failure, still, sin will always bring forth very negative results. But yet, as should be obvious, God looks at such a person in a different light than He does those who are engaging in willful sin. Both Paul and Achan are perfect examples.

I hardly think that any believer would think that the Lord looked upon Paul at this particular time of his life in the same manner that He looked at Achan during the time of Joshua. I make this statement even though Paul was sinning, and sinning greatly, whatever the sin may have been. To be sure, we have this scenario played out before us presently even on a daily basis.

Let us say it again: Achan engaged in willful sin, while Paul engaged in unwillful sin. But yet, let not the believer think that simply because it is unwillful sin that God overlooks the situation. The party is still guilty, and the end result is going to be extremely hurtful. In fact, even though it is unwillful sin in such a life, the situation will get worse and worse, with the sin becoming more and more pronounced.

## THE ONLY ANSWER FOR SIN IS
## THE CROSS OF CHRIST

Whether it's willful sin or unwillful sin, there is no other solution for this problem but the Cross of Christ. To walk in victory, the believer must place his faith exclusively in Christ and the Cross, which, at the same time means that such a believer must denounce everything else. While I love the church to which I belong, still, it, within itself, as an institution cannot give me one iota of victory over sin. While Christian disciplines are necessary for the believer, no matter how faithfully engaged, they will present no victory whatsoever. While manifestations of the Holy Spirit are desirable, still, as wonderful as they are, they will bring about no victory.

It is only faith in Christ and what He has done for us at the

Cross that will bring about the desired results. I might quickly add that it must be faith on a continuing, even daily, basis. The Holy Spirit alone can make our lives what they ought to be, and He works exclusively within the framework of the finished work of Christ. He doesn't demand much of us, but He does demand that our faith be totally and completely in Christ and the Cross and nothing else (Rom. 6:1-14; 8:1-11; I Cor. 1:17-18, 23; 2:2; Gal. 6:14; Col. 2:10-15).

## WHY WOULD ANYONE BE AN ENEMY OF THE CROSS?

The reasons are, I suppose, as many and varied as there are rejecters of the Cross. It's not an easy thing to reject the Cross simply because the story of the Cross is the story of the Bible, as the story of the Bible is the story of the Cross.

We receive many letters and emails in opposition to our position as it regards the Cross of Christ and it being the only avenue of victory for the child of God. Still, most of these individuals, whomever they might be, attack us personally instead of the doctrine that we espouse. While some make a feeble attempt to denigrate the doctrine of the Cross, most don't even try simply because, as stated, the story of the Cross is the story of the entirety of the Bible.

This automatically states that such individuals are not really attempting to live according to the Word of God, but rather according to some other word, whether developed by someone else or of themselves.

## ELIMINATING THE SPIRITUAL CRUTCH

For starters, the Cross of Christ eliminates all spiritual crutches. It cuts the legs out from under good works, denominationalism, and a myriad of other things that one might be able to name. It lays all of that waste. In respect to this, Paul said:

*"Yes doubtless, and I count all things but loss for the excellency of the knowledge of Christ Jesus my Lord* (the knowledge of the Lord Jesus which Paul gained through the experience of intimate companionship and communion with Him)*: for Whom I have suffered the loss of all things* ('for whose sake I have been caused to forfeit')*, and do count them but dung, that I may win Christ* (next to Christ, everything else is nothing),

*"And be found in Him* (to be united with Christ by a living faith, which has as its object the Cross of Christ)*, not having my own righteousness* ('not having any righteousness which can be called my own')*, which is of the Law* (pertains to Law-keeping; he was done with that)*, but that which is through the faith of Christ* (what He did at the Cross)*, the righteousness which is of God by faith* (a spotless righteousness made possible by the Cross and imputed by God to all who exhibit faith in Christ and the Cross)*"* (Phil. 3:8-9).

## CHRIST AND THE CROSS

The apostle then said, *"That I may know Him* (referring

to what Christ did at the Cross), *and the power of His res-urrection* (refers to being raised with Him in 'newness of life' [Rom. 6:3-5]), *and the fellowship of His sufferings* (regarding our trust and faith placed in what He did for us at the Cross), *being made conformable unto His death* (to conform to what He did for us at the Cross, understanding that this is the only means of salvation and sanctification)" (Phil. 3:10).

When Paul spoke of the loss of all things, he was referring to many things — his family, the place and position that he once had and held as a Pharisee, actually, once held in high esteem by the ruling hierarchy of Israel, etc. All of that had to go and go completely. Most religious leaders are not willing to do that.

It is sad, but many preachers, if not most, seek to gain the plaudits of fellow preachers, whom they desire to impress. As a result, they compromise the Word of God!

Paul set the example for us. We can please God, or we can please men, but we can't please both. Concerning this, Jesus said:

*"But in vain they do worship Me* (worship that was not accepted by God, indicative of much of the modern church as well!), *teaching for doctrines the commandments of men* (anything that adds to or takes away from the Word of God)" (Mat. 15:9).

> *Glory be to Him who loved us,*
> *Washed us from each sinful stain;*
> *Glory be to Him who made us,*

*Priests and kings with Him to reign;*
*Glory, worship, laud and blessing,*
*To the Lamb who once was slain.*

*Glory, worship, laud and blessing,*
*Thus the choir triumphant sings:*
*Honor, riches, power, dominion,*
*Does its praise creation brings;*
*You are worthy, You are worthy,*
*Lord of Lords, and King of Kings.*

*Glory to the King of angels,*
*Glory to the Church's King,*
*Glory to the King of nations,*
*Heaven and earth His praises sing;*
*Glory ever and forever,*
*To the King of glory bring.*

*Glory be to You, O Father,*
*Glory be to You, O Son,*
*Glory be to You, O Spirit,*
*Glory be to God alone,*
*As it was, it is now, and shall be,*
*While the endless ages run.*

# God's Answer to Fear, Depression, and Discouragement

CHAPTER 5

# THE FORCE OF FEAR

# THE FORCE OF FEAR

IF MY MEMORY BANK is halfway accurate, it must have been about 1997. I don't think I had slept a wink that night. We owed approximately a million dollars in bills that were then due, and we didn't have one dime to pay those bills. As stated, I tossed and turned all night long, extremely concerned about the situation, but not knowing what to do.

Fear is a powerful factor in the heart and life of any individual if allowed to run its course. It can cause certain types of sickness, nervous disorders, and emotional disturbances, and if allowed to go the limit, it can kill you.

They tell us that there are 80 types of fear or phobias that plague mankind. Ironically and beautifully enough, the Bible mentions fear 80 times as well. Is it possible that the Holy Spirit has an answer for every type of fear? No doubt, He does!

Unable to sleep, I remember getting up about daylight that morning. It was Saturday. Just as I was about to take a shower, I absent-mindedly turned on the radio, which was tuned to our station owned by the ministry. I don't remember the song that was playing, but I do remember that all of a sudden, the Spirit of God filled the room. It was so obvious that there was absolutely no doubt as to what it was.

I don't remember the song that was playing, but I definitely do remember what happened next.

## DO YOU THINK I'M GOING TO FORSAKE YOU NOW?

The Lord spoke to my heart. He said to me, "I've brought you through demons! I've brought you through the powers of darkness! I've brought you through Satan himself! I've brought you through your own stupidity! I've brought you through false brethren!" Then He said, "Do you think I'm going to let you fall down now?"

The power of God filled that room to such an extent that I had to tell Frances what the Lord had just given to me. No, I don't remember what happened regarding the manner and way we paid the bills. I just remember that they were paid, and we continued on with the work for God.

Stop and think about the following for a moment: Satan will tell you anything, just as he was telling me that day. We owed a million dollars, we were going broke, there was absolutely no way to pay the bills, and he was going to do us in, he intimated.

I suppose I can say without fear of contradiction that Satan has made his boasts to every believer who has ever lived. He is going to do you in! He is going to have you meet up with a car wreck and be killed, or at least laid up for months on end. He's going to drive you to bankruptcy! In fact, the list goes on and on. However, have you ever stopped to think that you are still here, and Satan has not done any of these things that he has claimed that he was going to do. I'll tell you why he hasn't done them—he can't do them! All he can do is blow and bluster, but you belong to God. You are bought with a price, and nothing can happen to you but that the Lord either causes it or allows it. Please understand that. Once you come to Christ, you are no longer out there alone. You have the Lord with you, the Holy Spirit in you, and there is nothing that They cannot do.

No sir, Satan does not do all of these things that he claims he is going to do simply because he cannot do those things. He can only do what the Lord allows him to do. Now, understand that. It's a tremendous statement, and it happens to be true.

Read the first two chapters of the great book of Job, and you will see what Satan was to do. He could only do what the Lord allowed him to do, and please believe me, it hasn't changed from then until now.

The force of fear is exactly what the phrase implies. It is a force, and it emanates from the spirit of fear. The spirit of fear concentrates on certain weaknesses in the life of a person, whether he is a Christian or not. Once the spirit of fear unearths the particular weakness of the individual, it will focus its entire attention on that area, chipping away at it, time after time, until the person finally succumbs to the influence the spirit wants to exert.

The person being attacked soon finds himself obsessed with thoughts of inadequacy, inferiority, insecurity, or whatever. This is the framework upon which this particular vulnerability to fear can be shaped. No one is without areas of vulnerability. No one is without danger of demonic influence if he fails to armor himself with the knowledge of the Word, and the many ways that God has provided for us to overcome and dominate the forces of Satan. Fear is chief among those satanic forces.

## THE GARMENT OF PRAISE

I have already given the following in this book; however, it is so very, very important that I want to make certain that you the believer understand what God can do for you, and how you can overcome fear by the simple method that I am going to relate.

The Lord spoke the words I am about to give to the great prophet Isaiah nearly 2,800 years ago. To be frank, that which He originally intended has not come to pass even yet. It will not take place until the second coming of our Lord, and at that time, Israel will accept the Lord Jesus Christ as her Saviour, her Messiah, and her Lord. There will be a tremendous time of mourning over the entirety of Israel when they find out the One they crucified was actually the Lord Jesus Christ. They will realize the tremendous suffering they have experienced through the centuries, all needlessly. The great prophet Zechariah said that the entire nation at that time (the second coming) will go into mourning.

He said: *"And I will pour upon the house of David and upon the inhabitants of Jerusalem, the Spirit of grace and of supplications: and they shall look upon Me whom they have pierced, and they shall mourn for Him, as one mourns for his only son, and shall be in bitterness for Him, as one that is in bitterness for his firstborn"* (Zech. 12:10).

Then he said, *"In that day shall there be a great mourning in Jerusalem, as the mourning of Hadad-rimmon in the valley of Megiddon."*

And then, *"And the land shall mourn, every family apart; the family of the house of David apart, and their wives apart; the family of the house of Nathan apart, and their wives apart"* (Zech. 12:11-12).

In other words, this is the great repentance of Israel when they realize who Jesus really is and their repentance and acceptance of Him.

The Scripture then says, *"In that day there shall be a fountain opened to the house of David and to the inhabitants of Jerusalem for sin and for uncleanness"* (Zech. 13:1).

I think it would be helpful before we go to the main text that we desire to explain and include the notes from The Expositor's Study Bible as it regards Zechariah 13:1.

The notes say:

"In that day," occurs eighteen times from 9:16 through 14:21. This shows how precious "that day" is to the Messiah's heart. In that day, His victory over the enemies of His people will be great, but greater will be

His moral victory over His people themselves.

The Christian's true triumphs are God's triumphs over him, and God's triumphs over His people are their only victories. Such was Jacob of old, who represented Israel in that coming glad day. The conversion of the apostle Paul illustrates the future conversion of Israel. He hated Jesus, but on the Damascus Road, he looked upon Him whom he had pierced, mourned, and wept.

## IN THAT DAY

The phrase, "In that day there shall be a fountain opened," does not mean that it is first opened there, but that Israel will only begin to partake of it 'in that day,' i.e., the beginning of the kingdom age. This fountain was historically opened at Calvary but will be consciously opened to repentant Jews in the future day of her repentance. For the fact and function of that fountain only becomes conscious to the awakened sinner.

A true sense of sin and guilt in relationship to God awakens the sense of the need of cleansing, and so the shed and cleansing blood of the Lamb of God becomes precious to convicted conscience. As well, the ever-living efficacy of Christ's atoning work, with its power to cleanse the conscience and the life is justly comparable to a fountain and not to a font. The sense of the Hebrew text is that this Fountain shall be opened and shall remain opened.

FOR SIN

To the house of David and to the inhabitants of Jerusalem for sin and for uncleanness," portrays the possibility that, of all sinners, the Jerusalem sinners may be accounted the greatest. It was Jerusalem that stoned the prophets and crucified the Messiah; therefore, great sinners may hope for pardon and cleansing in this Fountain opened for the house of David.

The entrance of Christ judges sin, unmasks its true character, and arouses a moral consciousness which approves that judgment. That entrance dominates, adjusts, disciplines, instructs, and cleanses man's affections, relationships, and desires. All of this must be cleansed, not only in Israel of a future day, but also in any and all of who come to Christ. That Fountain is open to all!

(The above notes on Zechariah 13:1 are from the scholarship of George Williams).

Now for the text of our study.

THE GARMENT OF PRAISE

*"To appoint unto them who mourn in Zion, to give*

*unto them beauty for ashes, the oil of joy for mourning, the garment of praise for the spirit of heaviness; that they might be called trees of righteousness, the planting of the* LORD, *that He might be glorified"* (Isa. 61:3).

Now you the reader may ask the question as to how this passage that really pertains to a coming day, actually the second coming, has anything for us presently.

First of all, let's pull out the short phrase, *"the garment of praise."* Notice the terminology. He speaks of a garment, and, of course, he is using symbolism, but the word *"praise"* is not symbolism. By the use of the word *"garment,"* it has reference to the fact that we are to wear our praises to the Lord as a garment. Now, let's see how it works.

## THE MIND OF MAN

I think one can say without fear of scriptural contradiction that sin begins in the mind. We realize that the Bible says it proceeds from the heart (Mat. 15:18-19).

However, when the Bible uses the word *heart,* the Lord is not speaking of the physical orb that pulsates within our chests. He is actually speaking of the soul and the spirit, and the mind is the gateway to the spirit. Man is a soul, and he has a spirit. While sin actually has its beginning in the mind, it cannot be carried out until it goes to the soul and the spirit, with the physical body then carrying to completion that which is first thought in the mind. So, we have a problem! (Rom. 6:13)

How do we stop evil thoughts from flooding our minds? How do we stop fear from filling our minds, much less oppression and depression? I'm going to show you how these things can be stopped, and how that it will bring a permeation of health over the entirety of your physical body, and above all, your spirit.

The mind cannot think on two things at one time. We may think at times that we can do that, but we really cannot. So, here is your answer!

## GOD'S WAY

Every time you think of the Lord or anything about His work or Word, then subconsciously start to praise Him. Just keep praising Him as long as your mind is in that channel, and you will find that fear cannot remain, oppression cannot remain, depression cannot remain, unbelief cannot remain, etc.

You don't have to say it out loud, even as you praise the Lord. You can say it under your breath, actually in your spirit. This floods your physical body, along with your soul and spirit, as stated, with the good things of the Lord. That's why the Holy Spirit through the great prophet Isaiah said that we could have the garment of praise for the spirit of heaviness.

Now, to look at the second part, *"the spirit of heaviness"* is fear, contention, worry, anxiety, etc. However, when you begin to subconsciously praise the Lord, you will find those things dissipating.

As well, you will find out something else. As you become

more and more accustomed to doing what I am saying, you will find yourself praising the Lord without really being aware of it. Please understand that your praises to the Lord will bring about health, will bring about security, and will bring about power. It will result in a sound mind and will give Satan no room to plant his seed of fear and doubt. This is God's solution, and please believe me, it works.

*All praise to Him who reigns above,*
*In majesty supreme,*
*Who gave His Son for man to die,*
*That He might man redeem!*

*His name above all names shall stand,*
*Exalted more and more,*
*At God the Father's own right hand,*
*Her angel hosts adore.*

*Redeemer, Saviour, Friend of man,*
*Once ruined by the fall,*
*You have devised salvation's plan,*
*For You have died for all.*

*His name shall be the Counselor,*
*The mighty Prince of Peace,*
*Of all earth's kingdoms Conqueror,*
*Whose reign shall never cease.*

# God's Answer to Fear, Depression, and Discouragement

CHAPTER 6

## INHIBITING FEAR

# INHIBITING FEAR

"I WAS WATCHING *60 MINUTES* on television sometime back, and the particular segment on which I would like to comment dealt with a problem that is not at all uncommon throughout this country (and the world for that matter). It had to do with people who are obsessed with a fear of people! Now, that's a strange term, isn't it, but it happens to be real.

These poor afflicted souls are afraid to go to the store; they are afraid to walk up to a clerk and ask for something; they are afraid to enter an elevator; and they are afraid even to walk down the street. Something within causes them to continually withdraw deeper and deeper into a self-imposed exile — a hermit's existence.

Without prompt help, the likelihood of their being cured is not encouraging. Eventually they get to the point to where they not only lock themselves within their homes, trusting others to bring them their necessities, but they even get to the point where they will restrict their activities within the house, setting up favorite rooms out from which they rarely venture.

This is a phobia. As we've said in the last chapter, we are told that there are 80 phobias as it pertains to fear. Also as previously stated, the Bible mentions fear some 80 times, and I wonder if it could not be an answer to each and every phobia. In fact, I know it is.

A phobia is a persistent, irrational fear or dread. It is precipitated and maintained by the spirit of fear — actually, a demon power.

As the staff of *60 Minutes* interviewed these people, they revealed the poignant tales of their inability to move out and cope normally with society. They told of cowering in a house, sometimes one room, gripped by panic at the mere thought of happening onto a confrontation with the public.

The basis of their withdrawal from society is the irrational fear that everyone they meet is evaluating and judging them. What is intended as a friendly smile is interpreted as a smirk. A solicitous question becomes a put-down. A friendly overture becomes a threat. Rather than living constantly with these imagined slights, it becomes easier to just withdraw.

The same situation sometimes leads to even further withdrawal into the world of autism. The autistic person takes his rejection of society even further, reaching the point to where he completely blocks out the awareness of people, even when in their presence. The autistic person lives completely in a dream world, having lost all touch with reality and having become a vestige. He is passive, unresponsive, and apparently unaware of anything happening around him.

## IRRATIONAL, PERSISTENT FEAR

There is an affinity of phobias with which people become afflicted (as stated, 80 types of phobias). They range from agoraphobia (a fear of open spaces) to xenophobia (a fear of strangers or foreign things). If we were to list the whole gamut between these two, there would be little room for anything else within these covers. The point is: Phobias are irrational, illogical, and pathological fears. There is nothing wrong with being afraid if a python or a grizzly bear shows up in your living room.

However, when you allow yourself to become ineffectual and incapacitated by groundless continuing fears, it is a sure sign that the spirit of fear has become deeply entrenched within your life. As we have previously stated, the only solution for this, and I mean the only solution, is the Cross of Christ. Fear that is a phobia actually is sin. The person becomes grossly interlocked with himself. Let us quickly say the following:

- Jesus Christ is the only way to God (Jn. 14:6).
- The only way to Jesus Christ is through the Cross (Lk. 9:23).
- The only way to the Cross is a denial of self (Lk. 9:23; 14:27).

Every one of us is attacked at some time with this type of irrational persistent fear. I don't care how godly, how consecrated, or even how scripturally knowledgeable the person in question may be, there will inevitably come, at least at some time, an effort by the spirit of fear to draw that person into bondage.

Satan with his broad-ranging and insidious methods will do anything to subvert and sabotage the healthy normal mind. Has there been sickness in your family? Has a parent died at a young age from heart trouble? You're probably going to die of a heart attack, too!

Is that logical? Is it a medically valid question? Not necessarily, but you would be amazed at how many people worry themselves into heart attacks because Satan stresses over and over to them that they will inevitably fall heir to whatever physical problems their parents had.

Now, I'm not dealing here with people who abuse themselves physically to the point where they are inviting physical breakdown. The person who abuses and mistreats his body to the point of physical disillusion would be well advised to be concerned about his health. Perhaps some well-placed concern might lead to re-evaluation of lifestyle and cause a reversal of the conditions leading that person down the road toward physical break down and perhaps even death.

## WORRY

However, baseless worry about health can lead to the very conditions about which the person worries. It becomes, in effect, a self-fulfilling prophecy, and Satan, as the source of these worries, knows this full well. This is why he hammers away at these areas, repeating and repeating in the ear of the subject scenarios of imminent catastrophe.

The person who is doing everything he knows to live a healthy and normal life — spiritually, physically, and emotionally — should reject these kinds of thoughts the moment they enter his mind. Recognize the source of them. Rebuke Satan in Jesus' name. Turn your mind to other subjects. As we have stated, begin to praise the Lord in your subconscious and don't stop. Keep doing it until your mind goes to something else. More and more you will then find that there is no room for unbelief, fear, oppression, etc.

Countless Christians refuse to enter an airplane. The mere mention of flying causes them to pale. Is this a normal reaction, especially for a Christian? No! In this day and age it is absolutely normal and rational to travel long distances efficiently and quickly by air. Still many, many Christians make travel painful or even impossible by insisting upon using alternative methods, and it's all because they're afraid to fly. This is bondage, and bondage is always from the Devil.

Once again, we restate the situation in that Satan cannot do anything to any believer unless he has permission from the Lord. In other words, the plane in which you are riding cannot go down as long as you are in it unless the Lord says so. If it's your time to go, you will go wherever you are. So, there's no point in worrying about anything, especially considering that you belong to the Lord. He who numbers the very hairs of your head and knows every sparrows' fall all over the world is perfectly capable of taking care of you. So, your worry and fear are bondages you don't need to deal with.

## BONDAGE!

The Christian shouldn't allow himself to be dominated, affected, or influenced by Satan. Jesus sets the individual free. *"Stand fast therefore in the liberty wherewith Christ has made us free, and be not entangled again with the yoke of bondage"* (Gal. 5:1). In this passage Paul was speaking specifically of bondage under the law, but the same passage applies equally well to any bondage, especially that promoted by satanic forces. Any fear, reservation, or apprehension that prevents us from dealing in the world efficiently and normally is bondage. Of course, I am not talking about dangerous, foolhardy, or reckless actions. Naturally, the Christian should avoid these, as would any prudent individual. However, an irrational fear that prevents us from flying, mingling with people, going over water, or crossing a bridge is certainly not within the realm of normal. As such, the person afflicted with these fears should face them, lay them out in the light of day where they can be analyzed, and identify their source.

God never intended for us to cower in a cave like an animal. He never intended for us to shun efficient methods of transportation. As well, He never intended for us to be oppressed by any type of irrational fear that interferes with the efficient, normal pursuit of our daily activities. When we allow ourselves to fall prey to these disabling factors, we become less efficient (or completely inefficient) in our daily life as well as in our Christian pursuits. This is why the Word tells us that *"fear has torment"* (I Jn. 4:18).

## BAD DECISIONS

I believe that most bad decisions — decisions that lead to unfortunate results — are made from fear. Nations and governments do irrational things when they allow fear to dominate their deliberations. If we were to go back through history and search out the causes of most of the wars that have been fought, I believe we would find fear of other nations as the cause of the vast majority of the wars that have occurred.

Throughout the world, there are millions today who are on drugs. I'm not talking about the "drug problem" — the rusty needle-in-the-back-alley type of drug taker. I'm talking about the well-thought-of executive, the socially acceptable suburbanite, and the loving wife and mother. These are the people who are daily ingesting drugs bought openly at corner drugstores with prescriptions issued by licensed, well-thought-of physicians.

People fall prey to these drugs and become addicted to them because they think they can submerge or calm their fears by hiding them behind the euphoria induced by drugs. The situation is such that it is a well-known fact that the late President John F. Kennedy was at one time in his life quite dependent on amphetamines (speed), to which he had knowingly been exposed by a physician who included large amounts of it in his "tonic ingestions." Is it any wonder that the average citizen then, trusting the advice of his family physician, is often led down the garden path, blindly accepting any prescription that promises to make life more palatable to him?

What about alcohol? Today Americans drink enough alcoholic beverages every day to float an aircraft carrier. Why do they do this? Is it because alcohol is delicious or refreshing? No. It's because alcohol blunts the concern of the individual and calms his fears, at least for a short period of time.

In fact, alcohol is referred to as "Dutch courage," whatever that means. The drunken individual will undertake things he wouldn't consider when sober. The social drinker endeavors to hold his conception to just that fine edge where he doesn't become sodden, but where he does manage to block out the fearful impulses being led by the spirit of fear. In both of these situations — drugs and alcohol — the Devil has a double-edged sword. If he doesn't get you with fear, he gets you with the *cure* for the fear — either the alcohol or the drugs.

The spirit of fear promoting the force of fear is so widely disseminated today, and so all-pervading, that no one is free from this threat. Naturally, those familiar with the Word of the Lord have an easier time overcoming Satan and his spirit of fear, but even they are not immune from this attack.

**INFLUENCED BY THE SPIRIT OF FEAR**

Everyone who draws breath is influenced in some way by fear. Fear is the factor that causes some men to be accomplishers, doers, and successes, while others spend their lives without ever quite rising to the level their potential would seem to promise. The difference is the ability of the individual to overcome and turn back the inhibiting force of fear.

Very few people even begin to approach the level to which their abilities could take them. We've all seen and been impressed with the rags-to-riches, Horatio Alger account in the weekly news magazines. We sit there and read about this one or that one who took a few dollars and within a few years ran it up into a great financial empire. After we read it, we sit back and think to ourselves, "I could have done the same thing." What is it that makes this fellow different from me?

What is it? Generally speaking, it's nothing more than the fact that the men who make successes of themselves are the people who have come to terms with fear and hammered it back into the mud from where it came. The men who do things are the men who look at the goal, not at the intervening pitfalls.

What about the average man — the one who has some ability, but just never gets around to striking out toward the goal he keeps picturing in his mind? It's fear oftentimes that keeps obscuring his vision. It's fear that keeps casting the shadow that blots out the picture of eventual success down the road. As long as your eyes keep focusing on the fear screen instead of the success in the distance, success will continue to elude you.

God meant for people to reach their full potential. He meant for everyone to utilize to their fullest the talents He gave them. *"Neglect not the gift that is in you"* (I Tim. 4:14). God never meant for anyone to be frustrated and held down by fear. Fear was fathered by Satan, who became, in effect, the prince of the world at the moment that Adam sinned.

Fear came into the world when Adam sinned and when fear entered the world, a choice became available to man.

Read the following very carefully:

- Trust
- Delight
- Commit
- Rest

Let's now look at the whole of these Scriptures, which give us the secret of God's blessings.

## TRUST

*"Trust in the LORD, and do good; so shall you dwell in the land, and verily you shall be fed"* (Ps. 37:3).

God's Word is full of promises — promises that are so bountiful, so miraculous, and so glorious as to defy all description. So, the first thing that you should do as a believer is put your *"trust in the LORD."* Then you are to *"do good,"* which simply means to obey the Word of God.

Most Christians never really give the Lord a chance. If the answer doesn't come immediately, they are gone. God cannot bless such. We must understand what God has promised, and we must place our trust in Him.

## DELIGHT

This passage is so beautiful that it defies description. It says:

*"Delight yourself also in the LORD: and He shall give you the desires of your heart"* (Ps. 37:4).

What is it in which you delight yourself? We are plainly told here to delight ourselves in the Lord. What does that mean?

It means that we have fellowship with Him each and every day in our prayer time. We do not miss this because it is of utmost significance. Then we are to trust that He will give us the desires of our heart. But yet, what you want must coincide with the will of God.

## COMMIT

He said, *"Commit your way unto the LORD; trust also in Him; and He shall bring it to pass"* (Ps. 37:5).

Once again we're faced with trust. We are to tell the Lord what we want but make certain that what we want is in His will. So, you commit your plans to Him, allow Him to move on your heart and correct you when the correction is needed. More than likely, it will be much needed.

## REST

*"Rest in the LORD, and wait patiently for Him: fret not yourself because of him who prospers in his way, because of the man who brings wicked devices to pass"* (Ps. 37:7).

We are here told to *"rest in the LORD,"* not in something else, and above all, not in ourselves. Then we are to exercise patience. Let Him work it out, which He will do in His own way.

King David wrote this psalm, and if there was any man who knew what he was talking about, David did. The Lord took him from herding sheep to become the most powerful man on the face of the earth. While the will of God may not be the same for you as it was with David and, no doubt, won't be, to be sure, God has a plan for you, and that plan is one of success. What is success?

Success in the eyes of God is simply being faithful for that and to that which God has appointed for your care.

## THE CROSS OF CHRIST

However, there is a trigger that brings all of this into focus. That trigger is the Cross of Christ, and above all, the Cross of Christ ever being the object of our faith. We must understand, and do so unequivocally, that everything that God does for us (I mean everything), all and without exception is made possible by what Jesus did at the Cross. In brief this means that the Message of the Cross is God's solution to man's dilemma. I might quickly add that the Cross is the only solution, with there being no other because there need be no other.

If you the believer will place your faith exclusively in Christ and the Cross, all of these great promises that I've just outlined for you will begin to take root in your life. However, if the Cross of Christ is ignored, you have just shut the door to all that God wants to do for you, and to be sure, He wants to do great things for you and with you.

Place your faith exclusively in Christ and the Cross, maintain it exclusively in Christ and the Cross, and you will learn how to trust, delight, commit, and rest in the Lord. However, without the Cross, you are not going to get very far.

Let me give you an example, once again using David.

## DAVID

When David prepared to bring the ark of God into Jerusalem, which he should have done, he never bothered to consult the Lord as to how the ark was to be transported. Consequently, he secured a new cart and placed the ark on that cart, which was against the will of God.

The ark of the covenant was to be carried on the shoulders of priests because priests were types of Christ. In other words, everything rests on Christ.

Because of David's folly, a man died, and to be sure, what transpired scared David nearly to death, if you'll pardon the expression.

But then, David was informed as to how the ark of God was to be transported. He, thereby, did what the Word of God demanded and placed the ark on the shoulders of the priests (I Chron. 15:1-15). Then he did something else that proves my point about the Cross of Christ. The Scripture says that when they were bringing the ark into Jerusalem the right way:

*"And it was so, that when they who bore the ark of the LORD had gone six paces, he sacrificed oxen and fatlings"* (II Sam. 6:13).

Six paces tallies out to about 18 feet. There is some indication in the Hebrew text that David sacrificed these animals approximately every 18 feet until they arrived at the tent where the ark of the covenant would be kept.

Those animals sacrificed were typical of the Lord Jesus Christ and the price that He would pay at Calvary's Cross.

David was made to realize that Israel's prosperity and power were totally dependent, one might say, on the Cross of Christ. It has not changed from then until now.

All of these wonderful things — these wonderful promises given to us in the Word of God — are dependent upon our understanding of the Cross of Christ. That great event made it all possible.

> *Come to this fountain,*
> *So rich and so sweet,*
> *Cast your poor soul,*
> *At the Saviour's feet,*
> *Plunge in today,*
> *And be made complete,*
> *Glory to His name.*

# God's Answer to Fear, Depression, and Discouragement

CHAPTER 7

## FEAR AND SICKNESS

# FEAR AND SICKNESS

FEAR CAN MANIFEST ITSELF in actual physical changes in bodily functions. Physical alterations aren't accidental or purposeless. God gave them to us to protect us in times of emergency, but here's where problems arise. When we live for prolonged periods with the body in the emergency state, harm comes to the physical body. This is why so many people are sick today. I am personally convinced that fear is the most common cause of sickness in modern man.

No, I'm not a doctor. I have never studied medicine, but like anyone else, I do have access to information. I believe that when the reader is finished with this chapter, you will agree with me.

A logical question would be, "Well, just how harmful can fear be to the physical condition?"

The answer to that question would depend to a great degree on how prolonged a period finds us prey to fear and how deeply we are influenced by it. Certainly, worrying about an upcoming electric bill never put anyone in the grave, but chronic anxiety can!

I read an article the other day that absolutely stunned me. It said:

"Many people have asked a question, 'Why have our scientists been unable to find a cure for cancer when they have been able to come up with such a glittering array of other accomplishments?'"

If men can walk on the moon with all the attendant problems, why is it so difficult to pin down the cause and cure for human cells gone awry?

Of course, the answer isn't nearly as simple as the question. To begin with, there are many different types of cancer. So, it isn't a question of finding a cure for a disease, but rather of finding a cure for a widely diversified family of diseases. This, of course, complicates the problem. The approach to different types of cancer will probably mean a wide spectrum of specific treatments once this dread disease is finally brought under control.

Even today, great advances have been made in treatments for certain, specific types of cancer, but a scatter-shot treatment for all cancers is a long way down the road, if it ever comes about.

The article then went on to quote one of the world's leading cancer experts, and here's what she said:

I feel that the basic, underlying cause of cancer is fear!

Every child born into the world has, within the myriad cells that make up the human body, a number of abnormal 'cancer' cells. But the normal defense systems built into the body by God deal with these cancer cells as they appear and prevent them from reproducing and becoming viable, identifiable 'cancers.'

But when fear, in a prolonged state, enters a person's mind and spirit, it somehow breaks down the ability of the human body to resist and throw off these malignant cells. They consequently gain the upper hand and not only begin to grow, but to disseminate (metastasize) throughout the body. When things reach this state, the prognosis for the patient is grave.

She went on to say:

I can't prove this theory. This is not a reproducible environment, and it is not amenable to laboratory controls. Nevertheless, I believe this, and if it were possible to duplicate the conditions we find clinically, I think we would find that there is a definite link between cancer susceptibility and emotional shock, particularly where fear is involved.

When I read this report, I was astounded; it literally shocked me. I had been preaching this in a vastly diluted manner for years. It thrilled me to see the scriptural warning, *"fear has torment,"* confirmed in this dramatic fashion.

## ADAM'S FALL

In Psalm 8:3-6, tremendous statements are made, and tremendous questions are asked.

*"When I consider Your heavens, the work of Your fingers, the moon and the stars, which You have ordained;*

*"What is man, that You are mindful of him? and the son of man, that You visit him?*

*"For You have made him a little lower than the angels, and have crowned him with glory and honor.*

*"You made him to have dominion over the works of Your hands; You have put all things under his feet"* (Ps. 8:3-6).

This is what the psalmist was saying: When I consider all that You have done, I have to ask myself the question, *"What is man? Is he just another pawn in God's great creation? Is he no better than the beast in the field?"*

Then the Holy Spirit answers these questions by continuing on from there. *"God made man a little lower than the angels. He crowned him with glory and honor. He gave him dominion over all the works of His hands. He put all things under his feet."*

Actually, in Verse 5, in the phrase *"a little lower than the angels,"* there is an incorrect translation of the ancient Hebrew word used, *Elohim.* In Hebrew, Elohim is a uni-plural noun.

In other words, in our language it would be words such as *herd, group, pair,* or *couple,* just to name a few.

Elohim means "Gods." A more proper translation of this

passage, therefore, would read, *"God made man a little lower than the Godhead."*

This may seem strange or even disturbing to some, but what I have said is correct.

This means that when God originally created man, He created him even higher than the angels and just a little bit lower than the Godhead. So, what is actually being said is this: God made man the highest creature in all of His great creation, as stated, even higher than the angels. It says further that man was crowned with honor and glory. There was no such thing as sickness intended for us. The human body, in fact, was constructed to live forever.

**EVERY SEVEN YEARS**

I chanced upon something in my reading the other day that impressed me tremendously. It said: "The human body replenishes or renews itself every seven years." What it meant is this: Although some cells (epithelial or skin cells, for example) are replaced far more frequently, the longest-lived cells that make up the human body (the way bricks make up a building) are replaced approximately every seven years. Thus, the materials existing today in my body or in your body are completely different than the materials that were there seven years ago.

While our bodies are the same bodies, all the materials in them (all the bricks in the building so to speak) have been replaced piecemeal over the years. Scientifically then, there is no rational reason for aging or for wear and tear over the years. In fact, our bodies should go on forever at the peak of youthful vigor and appearance. We should all look and act physically like 18-year-olds. Hopefully, our wisdom and mental powers would continue to improve over the years.

So, what has happened?

We know from the psalm quoted above, which is confirmed by the scientific fact of the replacement of cells over the years, that the human body should go on forever. The organs (the heart, lungs, liver, etc.) are constructed in a way that they should function eternally. Why then are we prey to disease? Why do we sicken and die? Why does even the strikingly healthy individual eventually fall prey to aging and senility? It is because of only one reason: Man abrogated the treaty set up between himself and God. God has never broken His word in all of time, and He will never break His word in all of eternity.

However, agreements (covenants) go two ways. Both parties have to respect them. Man desecrated the covenant God made with him. Man sinned when Adam disobeyed God, and this was the beginning of the dissolution of the world — and man. What we are seeing about us today is the ultimate consequence of Adam's sin and man's continuing preoccupation with sin ever since.

## CHANGED LORDS

At the moment that Adam fell, he actually changed lords.

Up until that moment, he walked with his Lord. In the cool of the evening, God would come down and walk and talk with Adam. It was a perfect environment. The animals were healthy, beautiful, docile, and tractable. Great storms never ripped across the countryside spreading death and destruction. The air was as pure as innocence itself. There was no pollution in it and no viruses or disease germs. There were no weeds, no thorns, no stinging insects, and no harmful animals, reptiles, or birds. Thank God, there will be a day in the not-too-distant future when this euphoric condition will return (Isa. 11:6-10).

Before the fall there was no such thing as fear. Fear entered when man changed lords. As Paul said (II Cor. 4:4), Satan at that moment became the little god of this world. At the same moment, fear became the dominant force in the world's system and thinking.

From Chapter 3 of Genesis onward, there is a striking change in mankind. As a matter of fact, the first words recorded by man after the fall were, *"I was afraid (fear)"* (Gen. 3:10).

Why was Adam afraid? Why should he have been afraid of God? God had never harmed anyone. Every good thing Adam had were gifts from God, and things haven't changed much over the years. Why should man be afraid of God today? Why should man be afraid to face God? There is only one reason: because man is the receptacle of sin.

With sin comes fear. When man fell, fear became the common denominator throughout all of humanity. It fastened itself to man like an inescapable parasite. It has caused horror, sorrow, and even the destruction of entire generations. It is, if anything, even more widespread and pervasive today than it was in the very beginning. The human body, despite the unbelievable complexity and fantastic engineering of its systems, can't survive the constant onslaught of fear, which is a continual part of the lives of so many people — even Christians!

## CHRISTIANS AND FEAR

The promises of guidance, help, and protection extended to the child of God are enumerable, but yet, not realized by many, despite being a child of God. So many specific examples could be cited that they would fill all the pages of this book, but just to point out one example, we can refer to Psalm 23. Any Christian who would engrave on his heart the words of this beautiful promise from God couldn't help but be happy, healthy, and strong in the Lord Jesus Christ. Considering that this is only one among so many parallel promises, it seems impossible that we should have such a multitude of Christians suffering from fear.

In fact, there is no need for any believer to ever experience fear, except fear of God, which is a healthy fear, and in which we all should engage. However, this type of fear (the fear of God) will not hurt us and will not strain our physical or mental resources, but it will rather have the very opposite effect. In other words, it will be and is a healthy fear.

However, I'm afraid that the fear of which we speak, which has torment and can cause all types of problems, is prevalent in the hearts and lives of many believers. It should not be, but tragically, it is.

## SYMPTOMS AND SOLUTIONS

Through the years in reading countless books and articles as it regards victory (victory over whatever), almost all have specialized in the symptoms while really never giving the solution.

In this book we have given many symptoms, but if you have read it carefully, you know beyond the shadow of a doubt that we have dealt with the solution. That solution is the Cross of Christ. Telling people how they act, why they act, or what they act, while proving to be interesting, does not really give us a solution. That's the stay of most material that goes out presently under the heading of Christianity. Most of it is an amalgamation of psychology and a detailing of the account without really ever giving any solution. I suppose the reason is that most don't know the solution.

All promises in the Word of God, and there are a myriad of promises, are predicated totally and completely on the finished work of Christ (I Cor. 1:17-18, 23; 2:2). If we don't understand the Cross of Christ as it regards sanctification, we really will not understand these great promises. In other words, if we don't know how to live for God on a daily basis, how we have victory over the world, the flesh, and the Devil, and how we grow in grace and the knowledge of the Lord, then we don't really understand what Christ did at Calvary. The key is the Cross, as the key has always been the Cross, and will always be the Cross.

## THE APOSTLE PAUL

If anyone studies the Apostle Paul to any degree, he will see that Paul was the masterbuilder of the church, meaning that God put the responsibility of the church in Paul's hands so to speak. Of course, Jesus is always the head of the church, but it was through Paul that the meaning of all of this was given.

- Jesus Christ is the new covenant.
- The Cross of Christ is the meaning of the new covenant.
- This meaning was given to the Apostle Paul, which he gave to us in his 14 epistles. If we study them at all, we must come to the conclusion that Paul's overriding message was ever the Cross of Christ. In fact, it's impossible to separate the Cross from grace or grace from the Cross. Without the Cross there is no grace. The Cross of Christ made it possible for the grace of God to be given to undeserving humanity, and to do so in copious lots. Without a proper understanding of the Cross of Christ relative to sanctification, fear is going to plague the human being. This is true even if that person is saved and even Spirit-filled, and even used by God respecting the gifts of the Spirit. That's

the reason that Satan fights the Cross as he fights nothing else.  It was there that he and all of his henchmen were totally and completely defeated.  So he wants the church to major in anything and everything except the Cross of Christ.

*Your way, not mine, Oh Lord,*
*Whatever way it may be,*
*Lead me by Your own hand,*
*Choose out the path for me.*

*I dare not choose my lot,*
*I would not if I might,*
*You choose for me, my God,*
*Then shall I walk aright.*

# God's
## Answer to
### Fear, Depression,
### and Discouragement

# CHAPTER 8

# CHRONIC ANXIETY, STRESS, AND WORRY

# CHRONIC ANXIETY, STRESS, AND WORRY

CHRONIC ANXIETY, STRESS, AND worry are considered by the medical profession to be the number one cause of heart attacks, strokes, and all other conditions related to the heart and the blood vessels. Going a step deeper, the cause of the anxiety, stress, and worry is "the spirit of fear."

Fear affects people adversely in two ways. One is through psychosomatic diseases, and the other is through psychosis. Psychoses are abnormal mental reactions. They are, in fact, the mind affecting the mind.

On the other hand, psychosomatic diseases are those that affect the body through the actions of the mind — the mind affecting the body. The term *psychosomatic* comes from two Greek word roots: *psycho,* meaning the mind, and *soma,* meaning the body.

It is hard to picture the mind affecting the body to the point to where it causes actual physical breakdown. However, it is a scientific fact that almost three-quarters of all visits to doctors in this country show no physical abnormality to explain the complaint of the patient.

This does not mean, however, the patient is imagining the problem. Psychosomatic (or psychogenic) diseases are as real to the patient, and as real in their effect on the patient, as any disease caused by a specific germ or physical abnormality.

Perhaps that's a hard statement to accept on the surface. So, just to verify it, let's turn for a moment from God's Bible to the "bible" of the medical profession.

All doctors turn frequently to a book called the *Merck Manual*. It is considered to be absolutely reliable and is one of the most widely used references in medicine.

The *Merck Manual* lists 16 separate and distinct common disorders, such as schizophrenia, and finally down to exotic diseases, such as anorexia nervosa, a condition where people actually starve themselves to death. Finally, it lists problems that touch almost every family in America, such as alcoholism. The important thing to realize is that the *Merck Manual* is not a psychiatric textbook. It is a reference book for use in the average doctor's office and contains the conditions likely to be seen by the average doctor on any average day.

Turning to the section on sicknesses and physical disorders that we might label as mentally induced, we find an impressive list. Here are some of them:

- Headache
- Blurred vision
- Noise sensitivity
- Insomnia
- Irritability
- Fatigue

- Dermatitis
- Eczema
- Rheumatism
- Cramps
- Coronary heart attacks
- Strokes
- Asthma
- Bronchitis
- Hiccups
- Ulcers
- Irregular or interrupted heart beat
- High blood pressure
- Migraines
- Indigestion
- Colitis
- Constipation
- Diarrhea
- Obesity
- Menstrual disturbances
- Impotence
- Urinary disturbances

Some might ask the question, "Do you mean that all of these things listed, or possibly more we haven't listed, could be caused by fear?" Yes, they can, and that's a medical fact!

## GOD'S CURE

In dealing with God's cure, I think we must go into a little detail to explain what the Lord did to answer man's dilemma.

That answer was and is the Cross of Christ. Any means or method other than the Cross of Christ is, in essence, saying that what God did was insufficient, and we continue to speak of the Cross.

So, Paul answers these accusations by saying:

*"Where is the wise? where is the scribe? where is the disputer of this world? has not God made foolish the wisdom of this world"* (I Cor. 1:20).

Paul draws these questions from combining Isaiah 19:12 and 33:18.

The question, "Where is the wise?" presents the first of three classes of learned people who lived in that day.

Concerning salvation for the lost (a solution for the human problem), Paul implies by this question that no human exists who is capable of thinking up a plan of salvation and victory over sin that will work.

This question would come home to the Jews who regarded their rabbis and the people of *"the wise"* as exalted beings who could look down on all poor ignorant persons or people of the land. In fact, before his conversion, Paul was in this very class.

He was probably looked at as the great hope of Phariseeism. His scholarship in the Scriptures (Old Testament) would have been profound, but yet, without their true meaning, simply because, for all his learning, he did not truly know God. Consequently, he did not truly understand the Scriptures and, in fact, could not understand them until he was converted on the road to Damascus.

So, when he asked this question, it was a question that was very close to home and one that he understood possibly as few other men.

As well, this question would have been aimed at the Greeks who regarded none but the philosophers as wise.

## WHERE IS THE SCRIBE?

The question concerning the scribe pertained to the Jewish theologians of that day. They were the ideal of dignified learning and orthodoxy, though for the most part, they mistook elaborate ignorance for profound knowledge. Does it sound familiar?

Paul is saying that no human exists, even the scribe, who is capable of writing a workable plan of salvation and victory over sin.

## WHERE IS THE DISPUTER OF THIS WORLD?

The word *disputer* would especially suit the disputatious Greeks, who constantly were putting forth great (or so they thought) questions that instigated all types of disputations; consequently, this question concerning the disputer, as given by Paul, covered the waterfront so to speak.

The Holy Spirit through Paul shows that no human exists who is capable of perfecting a plan of salvation and victory over sin, even if humans could devise one, which they cannot. The problem is the same today as it was 2,000 years ago with

Paul. Man, and even religious man, continues to try to come up with means and methods that will address the problem of sin, but it is all to no avail. Let us say it again: there is only one solution for this problem, and that is the Cross of Christ.

These questions as given by the great apostle are meant to put to rest any and all philosophy, body of learning, psychology, psychological concepts, religion, secular education, political promises, or anything else for that matter, which claims to address the human problem.

## HAS NOT GOD MADE FOOLISH THE WISDOM OF THIS WORLD?

The heading proclaims that what God did in the sending of His Son to redeem humanity was all totally of God and none of man. In other words, the Lord insulted the wisdom of this world and its claims in the most graphic, open, and obvious way possible. He did so purposely because of the conceit of man. This included both Jews and Gentiles.

The great apostle then said:

*"For after that in the wisdom of God the world by wisdom knew not God, it pleased God by the foolishness of preaching to save them who believe"* (I Cor. 1:21).

## FOR AFTER THAT IN THE WISDOM OF GOD THE WORLD BY WISDOM KNEW NOT GOD

The heading means that the wisdom of God is so profound and is so above that of man that man's puny wisdom, even the best he has to offer, cannot come to know

God in any manner. In other words, God considers the intellect of man so nothing, especially considering that it is warped and twisted by sin, that God will not even respond to such.

These words might be written as an epitaph from the tomb of ancient philosophy and of modern philosophy and science (science falsely so-called) so far as it assumes an anti-biblical form (Lk. 10:21). Human wisdom, when it relies solely on itself, may *feel after God* but hardly find Him (Acts 17:26-27).

The Cross of Christ was and is the greatest display of the wisdom of God ever given to humanity. That great plan of redemption was and is greater than the creation of the worlds or anything else that man might name. For man, and especially religious man, to offer to the human public other than the Cross of Christ only tends to prove gross ignorance. The idea itself is ludicrous!

## IT PLEASED GOD BY THE FOOLISHNESS OF PREACHING TO SAVE THEM WHO BELIEVE

This particular phrase should have been translated, *"It pleased God by the foolishness of the thing preached* (as men esteemed it) *to save them who believe."*

Williams said, "God, by leaving man to his own wisdom, demonstrated man's folly; for he not only was incapable of knowing God, but man degraded God to the level of a 'creeping thing' (Rom., Chpt. 1) in ancient times, and in modern days to a piece of bread which he first adores and then devours (the Catholic Mass); and further, by offering him life and the principle of believing in opposition to the principle of merit, God demonstrated man's moral and intellectual corruption."

As we have stated, Paul is dealing here with that preached, which is the Cross, rather than the art of preaching itself. The Cross of Christ is not palatable to the world or acceptable by the world.

Paul continues, *"For the Jews require a sign, and the Greeks seek after wisdom."*

## FOR THE JEWS REQUIRE A SIGN

The heading presents a strange contrast. In fact, the Jews had been given the most far-reaching display of miraculous signs, and by the thousands at that, regarding the ministry of Christ in healing the sick, casting out demons, etc. However, these were signs the Jews would not accept, instead demanding some type of stunt (Mat. 12:38; 16:1; Jn. 2:18; 4:48).

The truth is that they would not have accepted anything that Jesus did, irrespective of how grand or glorious it may have been.

## AND THE GREEKS SEEK AFTER WISDOM

The heading means that the Greeks thought that such solved the human problem; however, if it did, why were they ever seeking after more wisdom?

Williams said:

The Jews demanded that the claims of Jesus Christ should be accredited by some type of physical wonders, and the Greeks (Gentiles) that it should be demonstrated by commanding arguments presented with intellectual splendor. Both found it difficult to accept as God, a dead man handing on a Cross, for such Christ was to them.

In fact, the Greeks were seekers, not doers. They actually did not know what they were seeking, but they gloried in the fact that they were zealous seekers. They even thought of God as wisdom or truth. Their great heroes — Socrates, Plato, and Aristotle — were thinkers. Therefore, they were ever seeking but never finding because they were looking in all the wrong places — basically, within their own minds. So what they produced was no greater than themselves because the creature cannot be greater than the Creator. Consequently, they were imprisoned in their own philosophy as the Jews were imprisoned in their own self-righteousness.

It is said that Socrates said, "There is such a thing as good, and there is such a thing as evil."

It is then said that his student Plato said, "There is such a thing as good, and there is such a thing as evil, but there is a great gulf between the two."

It is said that his student Aristotle said, "There is good and there is evil, and there is a great gulf between the good and the evil, and we do not know how to cross over from the evil to the good." However, it must be quickly stated that

Jesus Christ crossed that great chasm and did so at the Cross of Calvary.

In answer to this, the great apostle said, *"But we preach Christ crucified, unto the Jews a stumblingblock, and unto the Greeks foolishness"* (I Cor. 1:23).

## BUT WE PREACH CHRIST CRUCIFIED

The heading, even though short, is actually the basic foundation of salvation.

Even though it was necessary that Jesus be born of a virgin, be a miracle-worker, and be the greatest preacher and teacher of all, those things within themselves could not redeem anyone. Jesus as a good man, as a wise man, as the Messiah, and even as the Son of God could not save anyone. Yes, as God He could have done anything He so desired; however, the Lord will never do anything that is contrary to His nature of pure holiness. So, if man was to be saved, it would have to be the hard way.

It is only through the crucified Christ, with all of its attendant horror, humiliation, shame, and spectacle that men can be saved. In other words, Calvary was not something that just happened, but it was a determined necessity. Jesus came to this world to die on Calvary. It took the offering up of His own perfect body as a sacrifice, which alone God would accept, for the terrible sin debt to be paid.

The offering up of literally hundreds of millions of lambs as sacrifices in the previous centuries all prefigured Christ.

As well, all the ceremonial aspects of the Mosaic law regarding the sacrifices, sacred vessels in the tabernacle and then the temple, the feast days, Sabbath-keeping, circumcision, etc., all pointed to the expatiatory, vicarious offering of the Son of God.

## CALVARY

Satan attacks the Message of the Cross as he attacks no other. He has done it through modernism, intellectualism, and psychology, and he has attacked it severely in the Charismatic community in what is known as the "faith message."

Many churches in this particular belief system will not sing any songs about Calvary, about the shed blood of Jesus Christ, etc. They refer to those things as "past miseries." While they admit that such is necessary for one to be saved, they teach that thereafter, such is a detriment to the believer. To make the long story brief, they claim that their victory is in faith and confession and not the Cross. In fact, it is a misplaced faith and a misrepresented confession. In other words, their faith is really not in Christ, but rather in themselves, and their confession is really not in what Christ did for them at Calvary, but rather in their own faith.

They would pay lip service to what Paul says here about preaching Christ crucified because it is the Word of God; however, they would explain it away by claiming it refers only to salvation, with no bearing on one's sanctification. In fact, they have a basic misunderstanding respecting the atonement, which is serious indeed! Actually, they really don't even place the Cross in the position of salvation, claiming that Jesus went to hell and was born again in hell after three days and nights of suffering. So, people are encouraged to believe in a Christ who was literally born again, and in hell of all places. Of course, there's not a shred of that in the Bible. It is made up of whole cloth.

The truth is that everything hinges on Calvary — one's salvation, one's sanctification, one's constant victory in Christ, divine healing, answered prayer, the baptism with the Holy Spirit, prosperity of every sort, communion with the Lord, gifts of the Spirit, fruit of the Spirit, etc. In other words, the effect of Calvary does not stop at salvation but continues just as important in one's everyday walk before God (Rom. 6:1-14; 8:1-11; I Cor. 1:17-18, 23; 2:2; Gal. 6:14; Col. 2:10-15).

## UNTO THE JEWS A STUMBLINGBLOCK

This short phrase speaks of the reason for Israel's rejection of Jesus.

They had for centuries been looking for a regal and victorious Messiah who should exalt their special privileges. The notion of a suffering and humiliated Messiah, who reduced them to the level even of the Gentiles, was to them a stone of stumbling and a rock of offense (Isa. 8:14; Rom. 9:33).

*Stumblingblock* in the Greek is *skandalon* and means "scandal, offense, or the thing that offends."

## WHY WAS THE CRUCIFIXION A SCANDAL OR AN OFFENSE TO THE JEWS?

In the eyes of the Jewish leadership, Jesus was wrong on all accounts, despite the fact that He was right on all accounts. He fulfilled the scriptural demands to the letter.

First of all, He was of the lineage of David, which the prophecies had said must be (II Sam., Chpt. 7), going back to that monarch through Solomon on the side of Joseph, his foster father, and through Nathan, another of David's sons, through Mary. In effect, had the Davidic dynasty continued, Jesus, being the firstborn, would have been the King of Israel and, in fact, will be at the second coming (Rev., Chpt. 19).

He fulfilled all the prophecies concerning His humiliation, even as Isaiah had graphically prophesied (Isa., Chpt. 53). So, the crucifixion should not have been a surprise to Israel, especially considering that the offering up of every lamb, which they had done hundreds of millions of times in the past 15 centuries, was a direct symbolism and representation of that horrible event.

As well, if a Jew committed a death penalty sin and, in fact, was executed (stoned to death) and then as a further humiliation to his family, his body hanged on a tree, he would be judged as accursed of God, i.e., doomed to eternal darkness without God (Deut. 21:21-23).

Inasmuch as Jesus was crucified, even though they were the ones who demanded this execution by the Roman authorities, in their minds this meant that Jesus was cursed by God. The idea that someone like this could be the Messiah of Israel was unthinkable, i.e., a stumblingblock.

The truth is that Jesus was cursed by God, but not for any sins He had committed, for He had committed none, but for the sin of the world (Jn. 1:29). As stated, Isaiah spelled this out in detail (Isa., Chpt. 53), so there was no excuse for Israel not to know what the Messiah would be like, and what the Messiah would do.

In fact, the very reason that Jesus was a stumblingblock to Israel was first of all because of their turning away from the Word of God. They simply did not know the Scriptures, even though they trumpeted them loudly each and every day. Lest we point a finger at them, that is our very problem presently as well.

## AND UNTO THE GREEKS FOOLISHNESS

The word *Greeks* actually refers to Gentiles; however, Paul refers to the Greeks for the simple reason that they were the philosophers of the world, claiming to hold the answers for the dilemma of mankind, or at least sincerely seeking those answers.

Both alike, the Jews and the Greeks, had failed. The Jew had not attained ease of conscience or moral perfection; the Greeks had not unraveled the secret of philosophy, which within itself is a search for truth. Yet, both alike rejected the peace and the enlightenment that could only be provided by the Cross, which they had professed to seek. *Foolishness* in the Greek is *moria* and means "silliness and absurdity," in other words, not worthy of any serious consideration. The accent of profound contempt is discernible in all the early allusions of Greeks and Romans to Christianity. The only epitaphs that they could find for it were "execrable," "malefic," "depraved," "damnable" (Tacitus, Suetonius, Pliny, etc.). The milder term is "excessive superstition."

The word used to express the scorn of the Athenian philosophers for Paul's "strange doctrine" is one of the coarsest disdain, calling him a "seed-picker." It referred to birds that picked seeds out of manure.

Regrettably and sadly, the crucified Christ still remains a *"stumblingblock"* or *"foolishness"* to the majority of the world.

## WHY WAS AND IS THE CROSS OF CHRIST AN OFFENSE TO MANKIND?

The problem stems from two directions:
1. Man's proposed self-sufficiency.
2. The humiliation and shame of the Cross.

Looking at self-sufficiency first, we realize that it all stems from the fall. Man fell because of disobeying God in the realm of not believing God's Word, thereby, going in a direction that was not of God, i.e., the way of God. Consequently, man has been going his way ever since, thinking that he holds the answer or solution to his problems. It is the rebellion of the creature against the Creator, in effect, claiming self-sufficiency — no need of God.

So, a man's fallen condition is that he doesn't think or realize his need for salvation or redemption. He realizes that he has problems, even terrible problems, but he keeps thinking he can solve these problems by education, better environment, money, politics, brute force, or psychology, i.e., psychotherapy. The idea that he can't, even as the Bible graphically declares, offends him.

Throwing oneself on a crucified Christ, albeit risen from the dead, is that which he does not desire to do, and basically because he will not admit that he needs such.

## THE HUMILIATION OF THE CROSS

The humiliation of the Cross is still present in the world, even after some 2,000 years of ministry by the Holy Spirit; however, it is somewhat a different type of humiliation.

After some 2,000 years and the work done by the Holy Spirit, the fact of Jesus, the Son of God, coming from heaven and dying on a Cross is not so much at the present time a source of contention. People either believe it, or they do not. In other words, the Holy Spirit has somewhat softened the blow of the humiliation of the person of Jesus and the ignominy of His cruel death.

By and large, the humiliation rests upon the act of the person accepting Christ. Satan, who is the god of this world, opposes greatly that of which we speak — the acceptance of Christ. So, in most cases the sinner who accepts Christ is held up to ridicule. Many, if not most, simply cannot bear such ridicule; therefore, they refuse to accept the King of kings and the Lord of lords.

However, I remind one and all that what is a stumblingblock or foolishness today will not be such tomorrow.

Paul said, *"But unto them which are called, both Jews and Greeks, Christ the power of God, and the wisdom of God"* (I Cor. 1:24).

## BUT UNTO THEM WHICH ARE CALLED

The heading actually refers to those who accept the call, for the entirety of mankind is invited (Jn. 3:16; Rev. 22:17).

*Called* in the Greek is *kletos* and means "an invitation extended, invited."

Some claim that Paul is teaching predestination. In other words, they claim that he is teaching that some are predestined to go to heaven and some to hell, and there is nothing anyone can say or do about it.

One should understand that the very theme of salvation is *"whosoever will."* The emphasis, as originally stated, is actually on accepting the call because, in a sense, all are called.

## BOTH JEWS AND GREEKS

The heading actually stands for both Jews and Gentiles, which includes the entirety of the world. The idea is that the call is extended equally to all. The middle wall of partition between them is thrown down, and there is no difference (Rom. 9:24).

In fact, this is at least one of the reasons that the Jews hated

Paul. Being the people of the Book and the prophets, which meant they were the only people on the earth who were privileged to have the Word of God, they considered themselves above the Gentiles. The idea that they had to come in exactly on the same basis as Gentiles infuriated them. That meant that they would have to admit that they were sinners and needed a redeemer. This they did not want to do. As someone has said, "All ground is level at the foot of the Cross."

## CHRIST THE POWER OF GOD, AND THE WISDOM OF GOD

The heading readily sums up Bible Christianity.

To those who accept God's great offer of salvation through Jesus Christ, whether Jews or Gentiles, Christ is the great miracle of God, and the great knowledge of God one might say.

The power of God in destroying sin and death, man's greatest foes, constituted the answer to man's dilemma.

As well, the wisdom of God in devising such a plan of salvation stands out as the wisest and most remarkable plan of all time. It pardoned guilty men and at the same time vindicated and glorified the justice of God.

However, it is only the called ones (those who accept the call) who are privileged to know this power and be the beneficiary of this wisdom.

This is what Jesus was talking about when He said:

*"I thank You, O Father, Lord of heaven and earth, that*

*You have hid these things from the wise and prudent, and have revealed them unto babes:  even so, Father; for so it seemed good in Your sight"* (Lk. 10:21).

"*Because the foolishness of God is wiser than men; and the weakness of God is stronger than men"* (I Cor. 1:25).

## BECAUSE THE FOOLISHNESS OF GOD IS WISER THAN MEN

The heading actually means that which men take to be foolish and weak because with arrogant presumption, they look upon themselves as the measure of all things.

God achieves the mightiest ends by the humblest means. The gospel of Christ allied itself from the first, not with the world's strength and splendor, but with all that the world despised as mean and feeble.  He joined with fishermen and tax-gatherers, with slaves and women, and with common laborers.

The text does not mean that God is foolish, but it rather refers to that which men think of as foolishness.  It is rather the wisdom of God because the Cross of Christ is the means by which men can be saved for time and eternity, and there is nothing greater than that.

## AND THE WEAKNESS OF GOD IS STRONGER THAN MEN

Once again, the heading refers to that which men take to

be weak but actually is not.

The idea is that God infuses with the Holy Spirit those who actually are foolish and weak, and then they carry out great things for the Lord. Regrettably, for the greater part, only the broken and humble are willing to allow the Lord such access to their lives.

*"For you see your calling, brethren, how that not many wise men after the flesh, not many mighty, not many noble, are called"* (I Cor. 1:26).

## FOR YOU SEE YOUR CALLING, BRETHREN

The heading refers to the nature and method of our heavenly calling. The fact that the group of Christians at Corinth was composed mostly of poor people, and that they were called to the gospel by men who were, as well, not noble, was a further demonstration of God's judgment of man's assumed importance and wisdom.

## HOW THAT NOT MANY WISE MEN AFTER THE FLESH, NOT MANY MIGHTY, NOT MANY NOBLE, ARE CALLED

The heading does not say "any," but rather "not many." There are a few of the worldly wise, mighty, or noble who do accept the Lord, but most think of serving Christ as foolishness, or else, they feel the price is too high to pay. In the New Testament, at least as far as it is known, of such rank we have only Joseph of Arimathea, Nicodemus, Sergius Paulus, and Dionysius the Areopagite (Acts 13:7; 17:34).

If one is to notice, Paul mentioned *"wise men after the flesh,"* which means they were wise in the things of the world but not in the things of God.

Those who hear the call are alone the truly wise, but they are not wise with a carnal wisdom — not wise as men count wisdom. They have but little of the wisdom of the serpent and little of the wisdom of this age.

The Sanhedrin looked down on the apostles as un-learned and ignorant men (Acts 4:13). "God," says Augustine, "caught orators by fishermen, and not fishermen by orators."

All of this was a frequent taunt against Christians, but they made it their boasts. Christianity came to redeem and elevate, not the few, but the many, and the many must ever be the weak and the humble. Hence, Christ called fisherman as His apostles and was known as the friend of publicans and sinners. In fact, very few of the rulers believed on Him (Jn. 7:48).

Again I emphasize that the strength of the text proclaims the fact that all are called, i.e., are extended an invitation, but only a few accept. In fact, in comparison to the whole, only a few of the poor truly accept and, as stated here, only a tiny, tiny few of the mighty and noble.

*"But God has chosen the foolish things of the world to confound the wise; and God has chosen the weak things of the world to confound the things which are mighty"* (I Cor. 1:27).

## BUT GOD HAS CHOSEN THE FOOLISH THINGS OF THE WORLD TO CONFOUND THE WISE

The heading tells us some things about how God works in this great plan of salvation.

First of all, it tells us that God deliberately and with forethought chose this particular plan, which means that it will carry through to victory without fail. In particular, the victory will be over fear, depression, and discouragement.

### WHY DID GOD CHOOSE THIS TYPE OF PLAN?

First of all, the system that produces the wise, mighty, and noble is not of God. It is rather, as stated, the "wisdom of the serpent" and "the wisdom of this age." It portrays the very finest that Satan has to offer. As a result, not only does it deceive those few who are in this category, but it deceives the masses, as well, because they aspire to be like their heroes, idols, etc.

Consequently, it is common to hear various people refer to the rich and the famous by saying, "He made it" or "She has reached the top." One longs to ask the question, "Made what?" or "Reached the top of what?"

While it is not true that all would have to give up their place and position if they came to Christ, still, many would. The manner in which some make their money or gain their place and position is contrary to the Word of God; therefore, even though at times God deals with these people greatly, most — in fact, virtually all — refuse that call. Pontius Pilate is a perfect example, along with Felix and King Agrippa (Acts 24:25; 26:27-28).

The terrible bane is that the modern church has compromised the message. They pretty much tell any and all that they can live any way they desire and remain in any type of environment and still be a Christian. Consequently, the name *Christian* means very little anymore!

## A BIBLE CHRISTIAN

While a person definitely can be a Christian in any environment, if that environment is ungodly, it is almost impossible for one to not allow the environment to get into him. It is similar to a ship that is on the water. As long as the water doesn't get in the ship, it remains a valuable piece of equipment, bringing sustenance and life to those in need. However, if the water gets into the ship, things are going to be damaged, and if enough water gets into the ship, it will sink. So it is with the Christian!

The Christian is in the world, but he must not be of the world. To the degree the world is in the Christian, to that degree will there be damage. If there is enough of the world in the Christian, the Christian can sink, lose his way, and consequently, his soul.

## AND GOD HAS CHOSEN THE WEAK THINGS OF THE WORLD TO CONFOUND THE THINGS WHICH ARE MIGHTY

God calls all and accepts all who come to Him, irrespective

of how foolish, simple, wicked, or weak they may be. All are accepted on the same basis, which is faith in Christ. As well, this alone hinders many of the noble for the simple reason that most balk at the idea of having to humble themselves even as the low and lowly. God doesn't have a first-class section, business-class section, or tourist-class section as do most airplanes. All come on the same basis, and all are treated in the same manner.

## THE SYSTEM OF THE WORLD

The system of the world is the survival of the fittest. That holds true not only in the animal kingdom, which suffered a change as a result of the fall through no fault of their own, but, as well, in the human race.

In much of the world, the high and mighty take advantage of the weak and helpless, and there is nothing they can do. One of the things that has made America great is that our system of government, which is based at least partly on the Bible, has attempted to address these issues in a fair and equitable way. In other words, justice for all!

But still, even in America, the poor get poorer and the rich get richer.

## GOD'S PLAN

As stated, the Lord receives all who come to Him. At the outset He makes new creatures of all, never attempting to rehabilitate what is there, for that is man's way. Incidentally, it is a way that cannot work. At the moment of the new birth, the Holy Spirit comes into the heart and life of the new believer.

Irrespective of what that person has been in the past or the previous deficiencies, the potential for great things now resides in the heart and the life of that person, irrespective of whom he or she may be. As stated, God caught orators by fishermen, not fishermen by orators.

Men are ever attempting to "make themselves over," "find themselves," or "find their niche in life," but never seem to succeed, irrespective of what they do. The reason is that there is no such thing as moral evolution. The truth is that self-motivation is not the answer. Man's problem cannot be fixed by a three-hour seminar. All of these things for which men seek can be found, but not in the world or the ways of the world, but only in Jesus and only as the Cross of Christ is embraced.

The Lord makes giants out of pygmies, winners out of losers, champions out of the weak, and masters out of the slaves. In fact, He is the only One who can do such a thing, and He has done it in untold millions of lives. He can do it for you if you have not already allowed Him to do so.

*Oh Saviour, precious Saviour,*
*Whom yet unseen, we love;*
*Oh name of might and favor,*
*All other names above.*

*Oh bringer of salvation,*
*Who wondrously has wrought,*
*Yourself the revelation,*
*Of love beyond our thought.*

*In You all fullness dwells,*
*All grace and power divine;*
*The glory that excels,*
*Oh Son of God, is Thine.*

*Oh, grant the consummation,*
*Of this our song above,*
*In endless adoration,*
*And everlasting love.*

# God's
# Answer to
## Fear, Depression,
## and Discouragement

# CHAPTER 9

# FEAR AND THE MIND

# FEAR AND THE MIND

AS PREVIOUSLY STATED, 80 TIMES in the Word of God we are told to *"fear not."* One of the classic examples of this appears in Matthew 14:22. It tells the story of the disciples attempting to cross from Galilee to the other side of the sea in a ship. Jesus wasn't with them. Scripture tells us that when the ship was in the midst of the sea, it was tossed with waves because the wind was contrary. In the fourth watch of the night (between 3 a.m. and 6 a.m.), Jesus went unto them, walking on the sea.

We are told in Verse 26 that when they saw Him, they cried out for fear. His answer to them was, *"Be of good cheer; it is I; be not afraid"* (Vs. 27).

This is a perfect example for life. As we strive to do the things that have to be done to live and serve God, there are times when the wind is contrary. It doesn't matter how much faith you have; it doesn't matter how consecrated you are; and it doesn't matter how well you know the Bible. As we make our way through life, there are inevitable periods when the wind isn't at our backs. The Word tells us not to think it strange when fiery trials come our way (I Pet. 4:12).

There is no way you can confess away the contrary wind. There is no way you can confess away trials. Satan is still in the world, and he will contest our every step and our every move. However, even though we can't eliminate the contrary wind, we can have victory over it. No doubt the disciples had labored all night long. Without a doubt their hands were blistered. They couldn't make a foot of headway despite their efforts.

## SHOUT AND REJOICE

How many times have you found yourself in a similar situation? You have a problem, and no matter how hard you try, there just doesn't seem to be any way out of it. Then, to compound your problems, you begin to worry about the situation. You begin to feel fear as you see yourself a helpless pawn, blown along like a leaf in a breeze, and powerless to control your own destiny. At this point Satan has control of the situation. He now has a perfect medium in which to incubate his mildew of fear.

The disciples cried out for fear. We've got many Christians crying out today. Unfortunately, instead of raising their voices in faith, many are crying out in fear. When you cry out in fear instead of in faith, you aren't going to receive any answer to your cry. This is why some Christians seldom receive answers to their prayers and why circumstances in their lives just seem to go from bad to worse. There's much wailing out to God, but it's grounded in fear, not faith.

What did Jesus say to the disciples? He said to *"fear not,"* but He first said, *"Be of good cheer!"* This is exactly the point I wish to make, and because of its importance, I will emphasize it again here. Whenever the wind is contrary, and whenever the night is darkest, that's the time to shout and rejoice. Is it easy? Certainly not. However, Jesus said to do it!

Are you to shout and rejoice after a whole night of rowing, after blisters have formed on your hands and then broken, and after everything you've tried has turned out to be useless, and you're not a foot further than you were when you started? Yes! Be of good cheer.

Then after we've forced our faces into a grin and shouted and rejoiced, what can we look forward to? Like the disciples, we can look forward to our Lord saying to us, *"It is I; be not afraid."* In other words, "Here I am, you've got nothing to be afraid of."

## BE OF GOOD CHEER

Is this something new and revolutionary? Should we be surprised when Jesus says to us that He is with us? We should not be if we've read the Bible. What believer isn't familiar with Jesus' statement in Matthew 28:20, where He said, *"Lo, I am with you always"*?

Knowing this, where is the excuse for harboring fear in our lives?

This is why He said the few things He said to His disciples

that night. They are:

- Be of good cheer.
- I am with you.
- Be not afraid.

This is, in fact, a commandment. The Christian has no basis for fear. He has no excuse for fear. He has no reason for fear. The song says:

*I care not today what tomorrow may bring,*
*Though shadow or sunshine or rain.*
*For Jesus I know, rules everything,*
*And all of my worry is vain.*

In John 6:21, Scripture tells us that when He entered the boat, immediately, the boat was at the land they were trying to reach. Whenever we meet Jesus in faith and victory, the problems disappear just as they disappeared for the disciples that night. This verse of Scripture is largely ignored, but it is a verse of great significance. What the Word is actually saying is this: In one of the most impressive miracles in all of Scripture, a whole ship, filled with people, was instantly transported from a point of peril to a safe harbor some miles away. Unquestionably, the sheer power of God transported it materially and instantly just as Phillip was transported bodily and instantly as described in Acts 8:39-40.

The Word is telling us in this passage: The things we're so concerned about and the things that cause us so much difficulty will be magically transported and transformed if we will allow Him to get in the boat with us. The Word is trying to show us that He can work out situations immediately! To put it in two words, *"fear not!"*

In view of the fact that we are told 80 times in the Word of God not to fear, am I then remiss when I say that it is a positive sin when we fear? Incidentally, as also previously stated, we are told there are 80 types of fears that plague mankind. Isn't it possible that the Lord has a cure for each and every fear, inasmuch as He mentioned fear 80 times in the Word?

## A PERSONAL EXPERIENCE

Going back to 1958, in the month of February, Frances and I were in Sterlington, Louisiana, preaching a meeting in a particular church there. At that time, Donnie would have been about 4 years old.

In the midst of the meeting, of all things, I came down with pneumonia. I was taken from the parsonage to the hospital and later transferred to another hospital closer to home. After a few days in that hospital, I took it upon myself to check out, and I went home.

Looking back over my life, I don't think I was ever so sick before or since. In all honesty, things looked grim. I was being attacked viciously by Satan right at the very beginning of my evangelistic ministry. I don't know how much Satan knows about the future, but he was certainly concentrating his forces to get me out of the way right in the beginning. Thank God, he didn't succeed, and I won the conflict on this occasion.

Please note here that I didn't learn anything from the sickness. I didn't learn anything from the trial. However, I did learn something from the victory!

## FOR WHAT SHOULD WE THANK THE LORD?

Today there are untold numbers of Christians all over the world thanking God for their trials, sicknesses, heartaches, and crises. They think (perhaps they've been taught this way) that they're supposed to thank God for their troubles. While it is certainly true that we're supposed to thank God for all the things He's done, there isn't any sense in thanking Him for the things Satan has done. Satan is the author of sickness and disease and troubles and trials (Acts 10:38).

Some might question this and say, "You couldn't have the victory unless you have the test and the trial."

This is true, but I'm not going to ask the Lord to send the Devil to me to inundate me with troubles just so I can learn something. The best way to learn is through the Word of God. The next best way to learn is from our own mistakes, but would it make sense to go out of our way to make mistakes just so we could learn from them?

## A CONTRADICTION?

While I suffered, flat on my back with pneumonia, my problems were compounded by the fact that there seemed to be a contradiction in what I was seeing before my eyes. I was trying my best to live for God and to carry out that which He had called me to do. My two cousins started out living for God as I had, but along the way, they had veered away from their commitment to the Lord, while I had done my best to be faithful to my commitment. I am sure that most readers will realize I am talking about Jerry Lee Lewis and Mickey Gilley.

At that time, they both had hit records with major recording companies. Money was literally flowing in like water. They had every material thing the human mind could conceive, and I, on the other hand (the one who had been faithful to his commitment to God), was sick, broke, and not even close to anything that could be described as successful.

One Wednesday evening when I was finally well enough to be left alone for a few hours, Frances took Donnie and went to a prayer meeting. As stated, Donnie was about 4 years old then. I remember that after she left the house, I picked up my Bible and was reading it. Then suddenly, Satan mounted an attack against me such as I have never experienced before or since.

## THE POWERS OF DARKNESS

The room actually seemed to grow dark and ominous. I felt as if I was sinking, descending below the surface of the earth. The air felt clammy, and there was an atmosphere of ominous dread in the room.

Then questions began to explode in my mind: How

was I going to pay my household bills? How was I going to pay my considerable hospital bill? How was I going to put food on the table for my wife and child? If I called myself a preacher, why had my God forsaken me? Where was He in my hour of need? What about Jerry Lee and Mickey? They had taken the other road, and they were making millions of dollars. And me? Not only was I without a dollar, I had no assurance of ever getting a dollar. I didn't have a single revival meeting scheduled, and there was no prospect of getting any scheduled. Maybe Mickey and Jerry Lee were the smart ones. Maybe I was the one who was wrong. If anyone needed proof, all they had to do was compare our situations.

As these questions flooded my mind, I suddenly detached myself to stand aside and look at myself for a moment. I found myself considering each question and then, with head down in defeat, mumbling, "I don't know, I don't know."

For those few moments, I was a captive in a black fog of despondency. Fear was attacking my vitals. If I had succumbed to it at that moment, it would have destroyed this ministry.

I looked around desperately, like a drowning man flailing about for anything within his grasp. Then my eyes fell on my Bible I had dropped on the pillow next to me.

As I clutched it, I didn't open it. I was crying to the Lord, "Please help me." I had never sensed the powers of darkness as I did that night. And then, as I called on the Lord, the Bible fell open in my hand as I picked it up. I know without a suggestion of doubt the Holy Spirit opened it for me because as my eyes fell to the page, they centered on Joshua 1:9:

*"Have not I commanded you? Be strong and of a good courage; be not afraid, neither be thou dismayed: for the* LORD *your God is with you whithersoever you go."*

## VICTORY!

Those are the words that leapt at me from the page. As I stared at them, they seemed to be set in more prominent type. They seemed to be illuminated. They seemed to stand out from the rest of the print on the page.

There it was! The Lord was telling me not to be afraid — no matter that Satan had inflicted me with pneumonia, and no matter that he had made such efforts to ruin me financially and in just about every other way. I was not to fear because God was with me. Furthermore, He was going to stay with me and go with me wherever I went.

Praise God! As I read those words over several times, the Spirit of God was so tangible in the room that I swung my feet over the side of the bed and stood to my feet for the first time in a long time. Once on my feet, I started to walk through the house, completely healed, with my hands raised and me shouting the praises of the living God who never forsakes His children. I went on doing that until Frances and Donnie came home sometime later.

I've never forgotten the lesson I learned from this experience. The Scripture the Lord held up to my eyes that evening is as vivid now as it was that night. The commandment given to Joshua that day is as applicable to us as it was to him. In fact, it is even more incumbent upon us to obey that commandment than it was for Joshua!

Why? It is because Joshua had only a basic covenant with God, but today, we have a stronger covenant — a covenant composed of mightier promises than those under which Joshua was operating.

What is our situation today as opposed to Joshua's situation?

How is our covenant stronger than Joshua's covenant? It is different in two ways:

Joshua didn't have the Holy Spirit dwelling in his heart exactly as we do presently, and Joshua didn't have Jesus' promise that He would never leave him or forsake him.

Therefore, if Joshua could obey this commandment and equip himself with strength and courage (be not afraid), how much more should we be able to do those things when we consider the extra assurance we have from God. If Joshua could demonstrate lack of fear with lesser guarantees, how much more is our responsibility to show our disdain for Satan and his spirit of fear.

*"Be not afraid ... For the* LORD *your God is with you, whithersoever you go."*

## TUMULTUOUS AGE

We are living in a tumultuous age, with one out of four people suffering nervous breakdowns or some form of mental disorder. This doesn't mean they're psychotic (crazy), but it does mean they are mentally ill to a greater or lesser degree.

We turn on the television or radio and are immediately inundated with one horrendous incident after another. We pick up the newspaper, and by the time we finish scanning the headlines on the first page, our day is steeped in gloom.

I was conducting a crusade in a midwestern city sometime ago. A reporter from the local newspaper contacted me for an interview. The last question he asked was this: "What do you think is the major problem in the world today?"

As I sat there silently considering his question, I asked God to help me with the answer. There is almost nothing that can't be included in an answer to a question such as this if you want to go on at some length. For instance, the nuclear problem hangs over the world like the Sword of Damocles, and the Muslim problem is proving to be probably the greatest problem we've ever faced. In addition, there's the human rights issue and world hunger. Once into this subject, where would you ever end it?

However, the Spirit of God spoke to my heart, and this was the answer I gave him that day: I said that it seemed to me that the greatest problem facing mankind now is the problem of uncertainty. People don't know what's going to happen. It's as though they are sitting on a powder keg with the fuse already lit but not knowing how long the fuse is. Man has lost his hope for the better day tomorrow.

When you talk about the majority of mankind today, you're talking about a group that doesn't know Jesus Christ as their Saviour. You are talking, therefore, about a generation that doesn't have a hope of a better day tomorrow. This is a generation of "eat, drink, and be merry, for tomorrow we die."

Anyone having the faintest spark of intelligence, who doesn't know Christ and who looks about him, doesn't have much reason for optimism. If the world isn't blown into toothpicks tomorrow or rendered lethal by clouds of radioactivity, it will rapidly be buried under layers of pollution and debris. If our savings aren't made useless by inflation, worldwide recession will, no doubt, render us all bankrupt anyway. Where, therefore, is the raw material for optimism?

## THE LORD JESUS CHRIST

Truly, the person who doesn't know Jesus Christ has little or no basis for hope, but what about us who do know Jesus Christ as both Lord and Saviour? Where do we stand? For the child of God, there is hope. It is even called *"blessed hope."* We know better! We know that the world is not going to be blown apart in a thermonuclear explosion. We know it isn't going to be vaporized in a cloud of fission or fusion particles. To the person drowned in the Word, we know the world is going to hold together until the day Jesus Christ returns. From that day forward, we know there isn't going to be any problem! Hallelujah!

We know the Lord is going to set up His kingdom on this earth and rule and reign for a thousand years. We know we will be with Him. We know it will be a world without want, war, sorrow, heartache, sickness, or trouble. With all these facts in our minds then, where is the excuse for being fearful?

Certainly for the person who doesn't know these things, there is ample reason for despondency, but we're not discussing them now. We're talking about the Christian who knows these things.

However, with this knowledge in mind, with no reason for fear, where do far too many Christians stand? Well, the doctors' offices are full, and the psychiatrists' couches all have waiting lists (and oftentimes with Christians as patients). Marriage counselors, financial advisors, child psychologists, and newspaper advice columns all reveal a litany of gloom and hopelessness. Unfortunately, as many Christians as anyone else are also chanting the litany.

## SOURCES OTHER THAN CHRIST

Millions of Christians are turning to pills to set their mood at the level they feel is desirable at any given moment. There are uppers and downers, supers, and so many other kinds of pills that it is impossible for anyone not actively involved in the drug culture to stay current with the nomenclature on any given day.

These drug-dependent people, Christians included, think the answer to their problems lies in a pill bottle: "Better living through chemistry."

The harried businessman can't face the day without his

Valium. Others can't get started in the morning if they don't pop a pill to start the battered and frayed machinery. They need an upper to start them off, and then they need a downer to shut them off!

This dependence on a series of pills for specific tasks at specific times becomes a vicious circle. Soon, all too many people find themselves so ensnared in this cycle that they go for days at a time barely remembering what they did. Many of them find that the only way off the merry-go-round is to commit suicide.

This is certainly not true of Christians! Oh, no? When Betty Ford, former first lady of the land, revealed that she was ensnared by drugs and alcohol, she served as an example to a hoard of American women who finally felt free to admit, if only to themselves, that no one is immune from the danger of such entrapment.

A recent newspaper article stated that the drug problem among American women has reached epidemic proportions. Naturally, the same can be said for men and young people, with the drug problem having now sifted down to the lower grades of elementary school!

Should there be death penalties for pushers? Is this the answer to the "white collar drug problem?"

**AFRAID?**

No. Unfortunately, every one of the tragedies I have suggested above is being played out today on drugs obtained through a doctor's prescription at the local drug store by a respected member of the community! This is probably the most tragic part of the whole situation. The circumstances and conditions prevalent today are accepted and condoned in every strata of society! People don't even blink their eyes at what would have been a scandal a few years ago.

What is the base cause of all of this? What is the foundation for these tragedies? What is the underlying reason? It is fear!

A mind benumbed by drugs may cope with fear better than the alert mind — for the moment! Of course, with time, that mind becomes permanently handicapped by the prolonged use of these drugs, and this is when suicide becomes a more and more attractive proposition. For the moment, though, the pill seems to provide a temporary answer to problems blown out of proportion by fear:

- I'm afraid I won't be able to sleep.
- I'm afraid this headache is going to get worse.
- I'm afraid I'll make a fool of myself in the meeting if I don't calm myself down with something.
- I'm afraid I'll never get through the day if I don't get a boost.

Never forget this for one moment: There is a dark power that has a commitment to take control of your mind. Satan is that power. You are, sooner or later, going to reach the point where you are forced to obey either him or the Lord Jesus Christ. The decision is yours — if you make it while you are still in full control of your mental faculties. Once you have relinquished the control of your mind to a pill bottle, the chances of having the force of will to make that decision is dramatically reduced.

*Hallelujah what a thought,*
*Jesus full salvation bought,*
*Victory, yes victory,*
*Let the powers of sin assail,*
*Heaven's grace will never fail,*
*Victory, yes victory.*

# God's
## Answer to
### Fear, Depression,
### and Discouragement

## VICTORY OVER FEAR

# VICTORY OVER FEAR

AS WE COME DOWN to the final chapter of this book, we want to look at the One who is able to give us victory in all of the problems of life, including fear.

God truly loves us and, as well, He controls all things, meaning that Satan cannot do anything to us unless it is allowed by the Lord. If we understand that and have that kind of knowledge, it reduces the fact of fear and, in effect, tells us that we need not fear at all.

## PLEASE NOTE THE FOLLOWING

Samuel Brengle, a gifted leader in the Salvation Army, wrote in 1918 of spiritual authority. He said:

It is not won by promotion, but by many prayers and tears. It is attained by confession of sin, and much heart searching and humbling before God; by self-surrender, a courageous sacrifice of every idol, a bold, uncomplaining 'embrace of the Cross,' and by an 'eternal, unfaltering looking unto Jesus crucified.' It is not gained by seeking great things for ourselves, but like Paul, by counting those things that are gain to us as loss for Christ. This is a great price, but it must be paid by the leader who would not be nearly a nominal but a real spiritual leader of men, a leader whose power is recognized and felt in heaven, on earth, and in hell.

When the believer places his faith in the Cross of Christ exclusively, he can then expect the help of the Holy Spirit, who will do great and mighty things in his heart and life. It is all through and by what Jesus did at the Cross. Hence, Paul said:

*"But God forbid that I should glory* (boast), *save in the Cross of our Lord Jesus Christ, by whom the world is crucified unto me, and I unto the world"* (Gal. 6:14).

John said:

*"And we have seen and do testify that the Father sent the Son to be the Saviour of the world"* (I Jn. 4:14).

- John was an eyewitness of Jesus Christ, both as to whom He was and, as well, as to what He was.
- He could testify as an eyewitness to the fact of the purpose of the Son of God. His mission was to redeem lost humanity, which He did at the Cross.

**AND WE HAVE SEEN**

Considering John's advanced age when he wrote this

epistle, the short phrase, *"And we have seen,"* probably tells us that he was the only one left alive in the world at that time who had actually seen Christ, had touched Him, and had been with Him for a protracted period of time. In fact, tradition says that in the last months of John's life, he said repeatedly, "When I'm gone, there will be no one left who saw Him, who touched Him, and who actually heard Him."

As John penned these words in his first epistle, his hair was now gray, and his skin was now wrinkled from age, but his mind was sharp as he remembered those glorious days. He along with a few other men had been privileged to walk by His side for nearly three and one-half years. During this time, there is no record that they ever doubted who He was. That He was the Son of God, the Messiah of Israel, of that, there was no doubt; however, at the beginning, they did not fully understand the purpose of His mission. It was hard for them to understand that He was both the suffering servant and the exalted king. As all of Israel, they wanted a conquering David. To be sure, this was what they would get, but not in the way they thought.

They wanted Jesus to conquer Rome and make Israel once again the leading nation in the world, but Jesus came to conquer sin, which was the greatest enemy of all. John now knew that beyond the shadow of a doubt.

## THE LORD JESUS

There seems to have been many in John's day who came

up with fanciful notions about Christ, but only John could say, "I have seen!"

And yet, as the Holy Spirit had the apostle use the pronoun *we,* it certainly referred to the apostles (all who were now dead, with the exception of John), but it ought not to be limited merely to them.

Every individual who is truly saved has the Spirit of God working in them. He permits us to "see" in the historic event of Jesus' death God's act for our salvation. Even though we have never personally seen God or Christ, we do see by faith that the Cross lifted up in Israel was for our sins and for our salvation. We do see in Jesus our own Saviour and Lord. We do see in the fellowship of faith the presence of His love. Because His Spirit in us gives us this "seeing" experience, we are commissioned to bear witness to the event.

## AND DO TESTIFY

The phrase, "And do testify," proclaims the fact that we must tell what we have seen.

Jesus said:

*"When the Comforter is come* (when the Counselor comes), *whom I will send unto you from the Father, even the Spirit of truth, which proceeds from the Father* (who goes out from the Father), *He shall testify of Me* (He will testify about Me)*: and you also shall bear witness, because you have been with Me from the beginning* (but you also must testify, for you have been with Me from the beginning)" (Jn. 15:26-27).

Therefore, since there is such a close connection between "seeing" and "testifying" and the gift of the Holy Spirit, it is likely that John meant his words to include his readers, and to be applied to all Christians now as well as in the past.

To what are we to testify?

In fact, as believers who have been changed by the miracle-working power of God, we are to testify to the entirety of the person and ministry of Christ; however, the emphasis must ever be on His sacrificial, atoning death. If we are to truly live and preach the gospel, we must live and preach the Cross (I Cor. 1:17-18, 21, 23). If the Cross ever ceases to be the emphasis of our life and message, we have then stopped living and preaching the gospel and have, in essence, made the Cross of Christ of none effect (I Cor. 1:17). That is the sin of the modern church.

## THE CROSS

In the modern church, the emphasis is not on the Cross, but rather on other things. To be sure, Satan little cares what those other things are, just as long as it's not the Cross.

Satan was not defeated in the healings and miracles of Christ, as wonderful and glorious as they were. He wasn't defeated by the greatest message the world has ever known that fell from the lips of the Master, as great as that was. As necessary as was the virgin birth, that did not defeat the Evil One. Neither did the perfect, spotless life of our Lord defeat Satan, even though all of these things certainly played an extremely important part. Satan wasn't even defeated by the resurrection of Christ, even though that put the icing on the cake so to speak.

To the contrary, Satan was totally and completely defeated by what Jesus did on the Cross and the giving of Himself in the pouring out of His life's blood. This satisfied the justice of a thrice-holy God and, thereby, atoned for all sin (Eph. 2:11-18).

We must ever understand that the death of Christ on the Cross did not merely represent a doctrine. In fact, it is and must be the foundation of all doctrines. Any doctrine that doesn't have the Cross as its foundation is not biblical.

## THAT THE FATHER SENT THE SON TO BE THE SAVIOUR OF THE WORLD

The heading presents an outsized statement. Over and over again, the Holy Spirit through John links the great sacrifice of Christ to the entirety of the world, which includes all time as well. It was John the Beloved who wrote, *"For God so loved the world, that He gave His only begotten Son"* (Jn. 3:16).

Then He said:

*"And He is the propitiation* (the One who satisfied) *for our sins: and not for ours only, but also for the sins of the whole world"* (I Jn. 2:2).

In all of this, John puts the entirety of the world on notice that in the eyes of God, there are only two types of people in the world — the saved and the unsaved i.e., those who have accepted Christ and those who have rejected Christ. This lays waste every religion in the world, every philosophy, etc. All is Christ, and more particularly, Christ and Him crucified. There's only one Saviour of the world, and that is the Lord Jesus Christ.

## SAVIOUR OF THE WORLD

The expression, "the Saviour of the world," has a reference to the fact that the Roman emperor was also called "the savior of the world."

No doubt, the Samaritan men also had the above in mind when they said to the woman, *"We have heard Him ourselves, and know that this is indeed the Christ, the Saviour of the world"* (Jn. 4:42).

Emperor worship was the state religion of the Roman empire and the binding factor that united its far-flung, subject-peoples together in a union stronger than that of any military force. Consequently, to recognize our Lord as the Saviour of the world instead of the emperor was a capital offense, for such recognition was a blow to the very vitals of the empire. In fact, that was the quarrel that Rome had against Christianity, and that was the reason for the bloody persecutions.

*"Whosoever shall confess that Jesus is the Son of God, God dwells in him, and he in God"* (I Jn. 4:15).

The confession is that Jesus is the Saviour of the world, is my own personal Saviour, and is the Son of God, thus, He is God the Son, thus very God of very God.

## WHOSOEVER SHALL CONFESS THAT JESUS IS THE SON OF GOD

The heading proclaims the fact that such is open evidence for the invisible inward union with God. Its substance is *"Jesus Christ is come in the flesh"* (I Jn. 4:2), and this is proof that one is from God, *"born of Him"* (I Jn. 2:29), or in other words, *"that Jesus is the Son of God."* It is not only an admission as to who He is but, as well, that He is that to my personal heart and life. When one begins to understand all of this, at least after a fashion, there will be no place left for fear or depression.

In this confession of faith, for that's what it is, we have not only the fact of who Christ is, but in the name Jesus, what He did, which refers to the Cross. Jesus is the Son of God, and this Son of God is the Saviour of the world. He is the only Son of God, at least in this fashion.

## THE INCARNATION

During the time of the early church, there were many false teachers who denied the reality of the incarnation. As a result, great stress was laid upon this great truth, and understandably so.

The incarnation was God becoming man, which was

what Jesus did. In those days, if one accepted the incarnation and the physical death of Christ to atone for sins, plus His bodily resurrection after three days, more than likely, that person had accepted Christ as His Saviour. In modern times, that is not necessarily true. Millions presently confess that Jesus is the Son of God, but that doesn't mean that they are saved, even though many of them may think they are. They have given a mental assertion of this fact, but they have never really accepted Christ in their hearts.

When one truly accepts the Lord, there will be a change in that person that will be evident to all. In other words, it will be obvious that that person has been born again. This means that merely confessing that Jesus is the Son of God, even though that is necessary, is not enough to be saved. One must surrender one's own life completely to Christ and understand that He alone is the Saviour. In such a surrender, one is born again, and with such a surrender alone is one born again (Rom. 10:9-10; 12:1-2; II Cor. 7:10; I Jn. 1:7-9).

## GOD DWELLS IN HIM, AND HE IN GOD

The heading proclaims the union of divine fellowship in which the Father is in believers and believers are in the Father.

Initially, John connected the fellowship with obedience to the command to love one another (I Jn. 3:24). Then he showed its dependence on the gift of the Holy Spirit, which definitely comes to all believer's at conversion (I Jn. 4:13). Here he shows that the fellowship is built on Jesus, who must be acknowledged as being one with the Father (I Jn. 2:23), as the One who came in the flesh (I Jn. 4:2), and as the Son of God who was sent to be the Saviour of the world (I Jn. 4:14-15), which He accomplished by going to the Cross. I am giving all of this about Jesus in that we might hopefully understand that once Christ is embraced as He should be, there is no room for fear, discouragement, or depression.

John speaks of God dwelling in the believer, while Paul speaks of Christ dwelling in the believer (Gal. 2:20).

However, the actual representation of the Godhead in the believer is in the person of the Holy Spirit (Jn. 14:16-17). As it regards the Trinity, to have one is to have all. However, at the same time, one cannot have God at all unless one accepts the Lord Jesus Christ exactly as John proclaims here, which means to accept what Christ did for us at the Cross.

*"And we have known and believed the love that God has to us. God is love; and he who dwells in love dwells in God, and God in him"* (I Jn. 4:16).

## AND WE HAVE KNOWN AND BELIEVED THE LOVE THAT GOD HAS TO US

The heading, in effect, says, "We have known and still know, and have believed and still believe." This John implies is back of our confession. To know as John speaks of knowing is to believe, and vice versa. No inner realization can be without a corresponding confidence, and no true confidence can be without such a realization.

As John uses the words, *"God has to us,"* it does not mean "to us" as it seems to mean, or "in us" or "in our case," but rather "in connection with us." God's love has succeeded in connecting itself with us.

The sequence of thought is this: First, we must know and rely on the fact that God loves us. Second, we come to realize through relying on His love (or having faith in His Son — the meaning is the same) that in His very nature God is love. Third, we discover that to live in God means to live in love. The fellowship we have with the Father and with the Son (I Jn. 1:3) — the fellowship in which He lives in us and we live in Him — is perceived as nothing other than a fellowship of love.

## GOD IS LOVE

The short phrase, *"God is love,"* finds John repeating from Verse 8. His wording is always most exact.

As stated, the idea of all of this is that God's love has succeeded in connecting itself with us through what Jesus did at the Cross, i.e., the expatiation of our sins.

All of this is connected to the Cross. The Holy Spirit through John is saying here that the way and means by which we know and understand the love of God (understand that He, in fact, is love) is by and through what He did in the sending of His only Son to this world, and Christ giving up Himself on the Cross in order that we might be redeemed. Philosophically or intellectually, it's not really possible for one to understand the love of God. It must be seen by and through the Cross, and if seen in that connection, it will become obviously clear.

As amply proven here, everything comes to the believer through the Cross. The Cross stands at the intersection of all humanity. By and through the Cross, man can know God, and a thrice-holy God can reach out to sinful man — but only through the Cross! "The Cross," of course, proclaims what Christ did there.

After seeking the Lord day and night for some five years (and doing so with tears) as to the way of sanctification, the Lord began to answer me. He took me first of all to Romans, Chapter 6. He then related to me in prayer, "The answer for which you seek is found in the Cross and the Cross alone!"

## THE CROSS

I will never forget that day or that moment. I knew instantly that it was right because it was biblical. From that moment, He has continued to add to this revelation, which, in fact, opens up the Word. It has wondrously and gloriously revolutionized my life.

I believe I can say without fear of contradiction that I know more about the love of God than I have ever previously known. Once the Cross becomes the center of one's thinking, then self ceases to be that center, which is the purpose all along. However, only the Cross can accomplish this fact. Any other direction leads only to more self, while the Cross leads to more Christ.

This Scripture tells us that God dwells in a light that cannot be approached by any man. As well, no human being has seen God in all His glory, and neither can one see such (I Tim. 6:16). When one says that "God is love," it must be understood that this does not constitute the entirety of the "being" of God. God is love even as He is light, but these things in no way totally describe who or what God actually is.

God is all of these things, plus so much more. But yet, none of these things do away with His personality. In other words, God is a person, which means that He has a personality.

## AND HE WHO DWELLS IN LOVE
## DWELLS IN GOD, AND GOD IN HIM

The heading refers to this great union being made possible by the love of God, which is made possible by Christ, which is made possible by what He did at the Cross. Everything always goes back to the Cross (Lk. 9:23; 14:27).

To help us properly understand this statement, it could probably be better translated, "And he who remains in love remains in God, and God in him." This means that all that John has said about the manifestation of God's love, and about the goal that it has attained in us, must at the same time be retained. Without the Son's expatiation, without Jesus dying for the world, and without our confession of the Son, this double remaining, so to speak, is impossible. When we confess the Son, it means that we know and believe this love of God. The *"double remaining"* refers to us dwelling in God and God dwelling in us.

The heritage of John's time may have talked as they pleased about God's love, while they denied the Deity and the expatiation by means of the blood of Jesus. In doing so, they did not remain in God, and God did not remain in them. This is still true with regard to all who are like them today.

## HERETICS

True fellowship with God is His remaining in us and our remaining in Him, and not a mere claim of fellowship. Because of its great importance, let's be clearer: For God to dwell in us and for us to dwell in Him, our faith must be in the Cross of Christ, and our faith must remain in the Cross of Christ. We can say without fear of contradiction that all of this hinges completely on what Jesus did for us at the Cross and our constant faith in that finished work.

The heretics of John's day denied forgiveness and cleansing from all sin by means of the blood of Jesus, and regrettably, their modern counterparts do the same thing presently. The modernists claim that the blood of Jesus atones for nothing, while the so-called Word of Faith people say the same thing. As the belief system of the heretics in John's day was blasphemy, the belief system of their modern counterparts is blasphemy as well.

*"Herein is our love made perfect, that we may have boldness in the day of judgment: because as He is, so are we*

*in this world"* (I Jn. 4:17).

## HEREIN IS OUR LOVE MADE PERFECT

The heading refers to confidence. This confidence relates at least in part to the coming time of judgment (the judgment seat of Christ), though John, as well, taught that confidence is the mark of a believer in every relationship to God (I Jn. 3:21; 5:14).

He may have introduced the judgment theme in the context of the commandment to love because Jesus Himself made this command so specific and established love as the basis for judgment. Not to love, therefore, is to disobey Christ and to spurn the Father's own love in sending Jesus. To live in love, however, is to live in God, and this results in complete confidence for prayer and judgment.

## HOW THIS LOVE IS OBTAINED

For the believer to attempt to perfect this love himself, which means by his own machinations, efforts, and ability, presents itself as a fruitless exercise. In other words, it simply cannot be done.

In the first place, this love of which John speaks is the God kind of love. That means the world doesn't have this love, and, as well, it means that it's not possible for it to originate in man. It only originates in God.

At the moment of conversion, the love of God comes

into the believing sinner. This is all done at the moment of regeneration, worked out by the Holy Spirit. In fact, it is impossible for the divine nature to come into the person without at the same time the love of God being a part of that divine nature. They are one and the same!

Does the believer truly think that God who is love, and who imparts that love to us (a love which is beyond compare), will allow fear, discouragement, and depression to become a part of our everyday life and living? Of course, the answer to that is obvious — no, He won't! So, if those problems persist, it's of our own making and not from the Lord at all. The truth is that fear, discouragement, and despair are to never be a part of the believer's life and living. Please understand that it is definitely possible for the believer to live above such things, in other words, to never be bothered by fear, and, of course, we speak of the destructive kind of fear.

## TO PERFECT THAT LOVE

So, the believer starts off with the love of God, which is automatically given to him at conversion. However, now the Holy Spirit sets about to perfect this love. Please understand that this is strictly and purely a work of the Spirit, which means that man cannot accomplish this task, even the born-again Christian. In fact, "love" heads up the fruit of the Spirit (Gal. 5:22-23).

So, if one automatically has the love of God at conversion, what is it that the Spirit is doing as it regards His fruit?

One might say that the seed of the love of God is planted in the heart and life of the new believer at conversion. The Holy Spirit is then to develop that seed and have it grow into a proper fruit. This is a process that takes time and cooperation on the part of the believer, but the great question is, how does the Spirit do this?

## HOW THE HOLY SPIRIT DEVELOPS HIS FRUIT

As we've already stated, it is only the Spirit of God who can do these things within our hearts and lives. It is impossible for the Christian to bring about any type of Christlikeness through his own efforts, personal strength, ability, or machinations. But yet, this is the great problem for the child of God. Most do not know how the Holy Spirit works and, thereby, try to see these things done in all the wrong ways.

As previously stated, the only requirement of the believer is that we understand that all things come to us from God through the Cross, i.e., the atoning work of Christ. Consequently, we are to anchor our faith in that which Jesus has done on our behalf in the giving of Himself in sacrifice and, in fact, not allow our faith to be moved from that finished work. Ever making the Cross of Christ the object of our faith (Rom. 6:3-14), the Holy Spirit will then work mightily within us, doing what He alone can do (Rom. 8:1-13). *"Herein* (and herein alone) *is our love made perfect."*

The following is a message by Miles J. Stanford, which I

think adds beautifully to the statements I have just made. We are indebted to him for the following:

## THE CROSS

Studying these truths is hard work, is it not? Although spiritual hunger and need are prime requisites for light and understanding, the Holy Spirit does not release the treasures of the Word quickly or easily. "Deep calls unto deep." We have to be prepared, and even then there is much time, digging, praying, meditation, yearning, and experiencing involved. True spiritual reality comes in no other way, but praise the Lord, it does come in this way!

Understanding and appropriating the facts of the Cross proves to be one of the most difficult and trying of all phases for the growing believer. Our Lord holds His most vital and best things in store for those who mean business, for those who hunger and thirst for His very best as it is in our Lord Jesus Christ. The believer's understanding of the two aspects of Calvary gives the key to both spiritual growth and life-giving service.

Calvary is the secret of it all. It is what He did there that counts, and what He did becomes a force in the life of a Christian when it is appropriated by faith

(Rom., Chpt. 6). This is the starting point from which all godly living must take its rise. We shall never know the experience of Christ's victory in our lives until we are prepared to count (reckon) upon His victory in the Cross as the secret of our personal victory today (Rom. 6:11). There is no victory for us that was not first His. What we are to experience, He purchased, and what He purchased for us, we are to experience.

The beginning of the life of holiness is a faith in the crucified Saviour, which sees more than His substitutionary work. It is a faith which sees myself identified with Christ in His death and resurrection.

## DEATH TO SIN

Actually, our heavenly Father has trained every one of us for clear-cut, explicit faith in this second aspect of Calvary, and I speak of our individual identification with the Lord Jesus in His death to sin and rising to resurrection ground.

The first aspect of Calvary concerns believing and appropriating the finished work of His dying for our sins, of which is justification. Now we are asked just as definitely to believe and appropriate the further aspect: "Knowing this, that our old man is crucified with Him" (Rom. 6:6): "Likewise, reckon ye also yourselves to be dead indeed unto sin, but alive unto God" (Rom. 6:11).

Our intelligent faith standing on the facts of Calvary gives the Holy Spirit latitude to bring the finished work into our daily lives. We stood on the fact of His dying for our sins, and this act of faith allowed the Holy Spirit to give us freedom from the penalty of sin — justification. Now, once we come to see this further fact, we are urged in the Word to stand on the liberating truth of our dying with Christ in His death to sin, which allows the Holy Spirit to bring into our lives freedom from the power, the enslavement of sin — progressive sanctification. And, of course, when we stand with Him in glory, we will be forever free from the presence of sin — entirely sanctified and glorified.

## OUR SUBSTITUTE AND OUR REPRESENTATIVE MAN

As our substitute, He went to the Cross alone, without us. To pay the penalty of our sin; as our representative, He took us with Him to the Cross. And there, in the sight of God we all died together with Christ. We may be forgiven because He died in our stead: we may be delivered because we died with Him (as our substitute, He died "for" us; as our representative man, He died "as" us).

God's way of deliverance for us, a race of hopeless

incurables, is to put us away in the Cross of His Son, and then to make a new beginning by re-creating us in union with Him, the risen, living One (II Cor. 5:17). It is the Holy Spirit who will make these great facts real and true in our experience as we cooperate with Him; and so the plague of our hearts will be stayed, and we shall be transformed into the likeness of Christ.

Through the crucifixion of the old man with Christ, the believer has been made dead unto sin; he has been completely freed from sin's power. He has been taken beyond sin's grip; the claim of sin upon him has been nullified. This is the flawless provision of God's grace, but this accomplished fact can only become an actual reality in the believer's experience as faith lays hold upon it, and enables him moment by moment, day-by-day, though temptation assail him, to reckon it to be true. As he reckons, the Holy Spirit makes real; as he continues to reckon, the Holy Spirit continues to make real. Sin need have no more power over the believer than he grant it through unbelief. "If he is alive unto sin, it will be due largely to the fact that he has failed to reckon himself dead unto sin."

## SPIRITUAL GROWTH

The Reformation brought into focus once again the emphasis on spiritual birth, without which there can be no beginning. What is lacking among believers to this day is the proper emphasis on "grow" — not just to be saved, and heaven by and by. What sort of salvation would we have if our Father simply saved us from the penalty of sins and then left us on our own to deal with the power of sin in our Christian life and walk? But most believers feel this is about as far as He went, and are struggling to get on the best they can, with His help.

And this is the Galatian error so prominent even now throughout born-again circles. We must be brought back to the basics; freed from the "penalty" of sin by His finished work; freed from the "power" of sin by His finished work; "justified by faith" (Gal. 3:24); "We walk by faith" (II Cor. 5:7); "As you have therefore received Christ Jesus the Lord, so walk in Him" (Col. 2:6).

We are not left to deal with the old life ourselves; it has been dealt with by Christ on the Cross. This is the fact which must be known, and upon that fact is built the New Testament principle and doctrine of holiness. In other words, Calvary is as much the foundation of sanctification as of justification. Both gifts spring from the same work and are two aspects of the same salvation.

Now, as long as the believer does not know this dual

aspect of his salvation, the best he can do is seek to handle his sins by confession (I Jn. 1:9) — that is, after the damage has been done! This takes care of the penalty of the product, but not the source.

Is it not time we allowed the Holy Spirit to get at the source and cut off the stream of sins before they are committed? Is this not infinitely better than the wreckage caused by sin, even though confessed?

When believers get sick and tired of spinning year after year in a spiritual squirrel cage — sinning, confessing, but then sinning again — they will be ready for God's answer to the power of sin, which is death to self, brought forth from the completed work of the Cross.

## THE SIN NATURE

When God's light first shines into our heart, our one cry is for forgiveness, for we realize that we have committed sins before Him: but once we have known forgiveness of sin, we make a new discovery — the discovery of sins, and then we realize that we still have the nature of a sinner. In other words, there is an inward inclination to sin. There is a power within that draws us to sin, and when that power breaks out, we commit sins.

We may seek and receive forgiveness, but then we sin again: and life goes on in a vicious circle — sinning and being forgiven, but then sinning again. We appreciate God's forgiveness, but we want something more than that; we want deliverance. We need forgiveness for what we have done, but we need deliverance from what we are, or we might say, we need to more properly understand the deliverance that's already been wrought for us by Christ. That's why Jesus said, "You shall know the truth, and the truth will make you free" (Jn. 8:32).

## SELF

Our reckoning on the finished work of our death to sin in Christ at Calvary is God's one way of deliverance — there is no other way because that is the way He did it. We learn not to add to the finished work in the manner of justification, and now we must learn not to add to the finished work of the emancipation. We will be freed when we enter His prepared freedom — there is no other. The believer can never overcome the old man even by the power of the new apart from the death of Christ, and therefore, the death of Christ unto sin is indispensable, and unless the Cross is made the basis upon which we overcome the old man, we only drop into another form of morality; in other words, we are seeking by self-effort to overcome self, and the struggle is hopeless.

I must recognize that the enemy within the camp — the flesh, the old nature, self, I, the old Adam — is a usurper. By faith I must reckon him to be in the place that God put him — crucified with Christ. I must realize that now my life is hid with Christ in God; that He is my life.

## THE CROSS, OUR FAITH, AND THE HOLY SPIRIT

The message I've just given you from Miles J. Stanford says it and says it well; however, as it regards the Christian who is unacquainted with the Cross as it pertains to our sanctification experience, I'm afraid that some of the statements as given by our brother need qualification.

For instance, he said that we learned when we got saved not to add to the finished work of Christ in the matter of justification. In other words, we were saved simply by trusting in Christ and what He did for us at the Cross, and we must not try to add works or merit to our faith. The entire scenario of salvation pertains to faith, but more particularly, faith exclusively in what Christ did at the Cross on our behalf.

Most Christians understand that, but as it regards the Cross, that's about as far as they go in their thinking, and it's simply because they have been taught next to nothing concerning the sanctification process as it regards the Cross. The believer must know and understand that every single thing we receive from the Lord, which includes our salvation and then our victorious walk on a daily basis, comes exclusively through what Jesus did at the Cross. Consequently, our faith must be placed in the Cross, must remain in the Cross, and must not be moved away from the Cross.

With this done, the Holy Spirit will then help us mightily and greatly simply because all that He does is done exclusively within the parameters of the finished work of Christ. So, if we want the help of the Spirit, which we definitely must have if we are to be what we are to be in the Lord, then our faith must be exclusively in the finished work of Christ (Rom. 8:1-13).

## THE FINISHED WORK OF CHRIST

First of all, what do we mean by the statement "the finished work of Christ"?

Paul said:

*"When He* (Jesus) *had by Himself purged our sins* (which He did at the Cross)*, sat down on the right hand of the Majesty on high"* (Heb. 1:3).

The apostle then said:

*"But this man* (Christ)*, after He had offered one sacrifice for sins forever* (which He did at the Cross)*, sat down on the right hand of God"* (Heb. 10:12).

By the Holy Spirit emphasizing the fact that Jesus has sat down on the right hand of God, it tells us that His work was total and, thereby, completed. In other words, there is nothing else that needs to be done as it regards our salvation and, in fact, all that we receive from the Lord.

These statements had to do with the old Levitical priesthood. As it regards all of the sacred utensils of the tabernacle and temple, there was not a single chair among these vessels. The reason is that the work of the priests was never finished. In other words, they had to continue to offer up more and more sacrifices because the blood of bulls and goats could not take away sins; therefore, it was necessary that more sacrifices continue to be offered (Heb. 10:4). So the work of the priest in the Old Testament system was never finished.

However, when Jesus came (to whom the sacrifices pointed) and gave Himself on the Cross, what He did was so total and so complete that it will never have to be repeated in all of eternity. In fact, Paul referred to His sacrifice of Himself as *"the blood of the everlasting covenant"* (Heb. 13:20).

Now, if what Jesus did is 100 percent sufficient, this means that we now have a perfect salvation and a perfect victory. That means that we cannot add anything to what He has already done, and, in fact, we must not add anything to what He has already done. We must get this in our minds and understand that His work is a finished work. So why am I stressing this?

## WORKS

Paul said, *"And if by grace, then is it no more of works"* (Rom. 11:6).

The apostle also said: *"Even as David also describes the blessedness of the man, unto whom God imputes righteousness without works"* (Rom. 4:6). He then said: *"Knowing that a man is not justified by the works of the law, but by the faith of Jesus Christ ... For by the works of the law shall no flesh be justified"* (Gal. 2:16).

When most Christians read these words, they think of salvation. Of course, they do refer to salvation, but they also refer to our everyday living before God. What do we mean by that?

The modern church is very bad about preaching faith for salvation and then preaching works for sanctification. They do it in two ways, both of them grossly wrong:

## SANCTIFIED BY WORKS

The church for all practical purposes teaches that one can be sanctified by works. In other words, most Christians think that we draw closer to God or become Christlike by doing certain good things. Believers believe this and try to do this because this is what they are taught.

However, we do not become Christlike by doing good things, as good as those things may be in their own right. To become Christlike means to get closer and closer to the Lord, which means to walk victoriously over the world, the flesh, and the Devil. We become Christlike strictly by evidencing faith in what Christ did at the Cross on our behalf. When we do this, even as we've already stated, the Holy Spirit, who works completely within the parameters of the finished work of Christ, then develops His fruit within our hearts and lives.

This is the only way that one can become Christlike, get closer to God, walk in victory, etc.

## PUNISHMENT

When it comes to sin, most in the modern church believe that in some way a Christian ought to be punished for failure, and especially preachers. Whether they realize it or not, they are, in essence, saying that one has to earn one's forgiveness, which is totally contrary to the Word of God.

In the first place, such an attitude loudly states that we need to add to what Jesus has already suffered, who, in fact, was punished on our behalf. I would certainly trust that upon proper contemplation of such thinking we would see how sinful and wicked that it really is.

Considering what Jesus suffered, and then for us to think that He didn't suffer enough, is an insult to Him at the highest magnitude. Whether speaking of a preacher or the laity, there's only one sacrifice for sin, and that's the sacrifice of Christ. To be sure, what He did at the Cross is enough to satisfy every single sin debt (I Jn. 2:1-2).

So, the idea of punishment is an insult to Christ to say the least. Anyway, one must hurriedly ask, "How much punishment is needed? How many stripes of the lictor's lash will be enough to atone for whatever is done?"

I would trust that the reader can understand how wrong

such a direction is.

In both of these points — works and punishment — the church is engaging in works, which God can never accept. This shows that they really do not understand the work of Christ as a finished work. If they did, they would dispense with the works and rely strictly on faith and what He has already done on our behalf.

## FAITH

Most Christians will readily state that they are "trusting Christ," which means that they have faith in Christ. However, the truth is that most Christians really don't understand totally what faith is.

Before we comment on the subject, let me first of all say that when the Bible speaks of believing or faith, without exception, it is always speaking of faith in Christ, and more particularly, what Christ did for us at the Cross.

Irrespective of what the statement may be, whether it's in the Old or New Testament, if we trace it back to its roots, always and without exception, it centers up on Christ, and more particularly, the sacrifice of Christ. In fact, that is the story of the entirety of the Bible.

So, as it regards faith, the believer must always understand that the object of faith (that's what is so very, very important) must always be in Christ, and Him crucified (I Cor. 2:2, 5). As I've said repeatedly in this volume, we must not separate Christ from the Cross or the Cross from Christ. To do so is to conclude by preaching and believing *"another Jesus"* (II Cor. 11:4).

## THE CROSS

Millions of Christians, who mostly have been taught wrong, keep trying to increase their faith. In reality, the increase of faith is not actually the idea. The idea is the correct object of faith. The correct object, as previously stated, must always be Jesus Christ and Him crucified.

To make Christ the object of our faith without including the Cross denies the very purpose for His coming to this world and the very cause of our redemption. The truth is that the Cross of Christ was a settled fact before the world was ever created (I Pet. 1:18-20).

Jesus mentioned to His disciples how that He must go to Jerusalem, *"and suffer many things of the elders and chief priests and scribes, and be killed, and be raised again the third day."*

When He said these things, the Scripture says that *"Peter took Him, and began to rebuke Him, saying, Be it far from You, Lord: this shall not be unto You."*

Jesus was very upset over the statement as given by the big fisherman and, thereby, turned and said unto Peter: *"Get thee behind me, Satan: you are an offence unto me: for you savor not the things that be of God, but those that be of men"* (Mat. 16:21-23). We learn here that any idea that turned Christ away from the Cross, which was the very reason He came to this world, was an idea fostered by Satan. So we learn from this that any denigration of the Cross, any put down of the Cross, or any misinterpretation of the Cross is, in fact, a misinterpretation of the entirety of the plan of God. In fact, all such thinking is of Satan. It cannot be stated any other way.

## FALSE DIRECTION

Please allow me to mention the Word of Faith doctrine, which I personally feel is not any faith at all, at least that God will recognize. It goes under several names, but this is, I think, the most common designation.

This teaching has had a powerful impact on the modern church. Because of its view of the Cross, I maintain that this doctrine is not of God but is, in fact, of the Evil One. In truth, it has caused more damage to the modern church than possibly any other error of the last half of the 20th century and on into the 21st century.

For the most part, this particular gospel, which, in reality, is *"another gospel"* (II Cor. 11:4), has degenerated into what I refer to as the "money gospel" or the "greed gospel." It comes back to this statement as given by Paul that *"a little leaven leavens the whole lump"* (Gal. 5:9).

If not corrected, any doctrine that's wrong will only get more and more wrong. The fundamental wrongness of this doctrine is its viewpoint of the Cross.

In other words, its not faith in Christ and the Cross,

but rather faith in self. It may claim to be faith in the Word, but it is a perverted word, i.e., the Word taken out of context.

## E.W. KENYON

E. W. Kenyon wrote:

We have sung "near the Cross," and we have prayed that we might be "near the Cross," but the Cross (he said) has no salvation in it. It is a place of failure and defeat. (Taken from his advanced Bible course, page 279.)

It is from Kenyon that Kenneth Hagin and Kenneth Copeland get their unfundamental ideas.

No salvation in the Cross?

Paul said:

*"Christ sent me not to baptize, but to preach the gospel: not with wisdom of words, lest the Cross of Christ should be made of none effect"* (I Cor. 1:17).

He then said:

*"For the preaching of the Cross is to them who perish foolishness; but unto us who are saved it is the power of God"* (I Cor. 1:18).

He also said:

*"We preach Christ crucified"* (I Cor. 1:23).

Then finally, he said:

*"I determined not to know anything among you, save*

*Jesus Christ, and Him crucified"* (I Cor. 2:2).

Now, where does that place Kenyon's statement that there is no salvation in the Cross?

## KENNETH COPELAND

Kenneth Copeland says in his reference edition of the Bible, page 129: "Satan conquered Jesus on the Cross and took his spirit to the dark regions of hell."

To put such a statement in the commentary notes in a Bible shows one's contempt for the truth.

What did Jesus say on the Cross? Did He say, "It is unfinished," or did He say, "It is finished"? Of course, we know that He said, *"It is finished"* (Jn. 19:30).

The term, *It is finished,* means "paid in full." This doesn't sound like Satan conquering Jesus to me, and I don't think it does to you either.

Copeland also said, "Jesus' death on the Cross was not enough to save us." (This is from his message, *"What Happened From the Cross to the Throne,"* Tape 000303.)

Concerning Copeland's statement, Paul said, *"Blotting out the handwriting of ordinances that was against us, which was contrary to us, and took it out of the way, nailing it to His Cross; and having spoiled principalities and powers, He made a show of them openly, triumphing over them in it"* (Col. 2:14-15).

What Paul said sounds to me like that was enough to save us.

## FRED PRICE

Fred Price, another devotee to the Word of Faith doctrine, said, "After He died spiritually, He (meaning Jesus) is not made alive (born again) until He suffers for our sin in hell."

He then went on to say:

Do you think that the punishment for our sin was to die on the Cross? If that were the case, the two thieves could have paid your price. No, the punishment was to go into hell itself and to serve time in hell separated from God … Satan and all the demons of hell thought they had Him bound, and they threw a net over Jesus and dragged Him down to the very pit of hell itself to serve our sentence. (Printed in the *Ever Increasing Faith Messenger* magazine, June 1980).

There are many things wrong with this statement, but the main thing is that it is pure fiction. The Bible has absolutely nothing to say about Jesus going down into the burning side of hell, there to serve time separated from God. It has absolutely nothing to say about Satan and all the demons of hell throwing a net over Jesus and dragging Him down to the pit of hell itself to serve our sentence. All of that, as stated, is pure fiction.

The evidence of Scripture is overwhelming in its

testimony to the fact that Christ's death on the Cross was a physical death only. There was no suffering in the burning side of hell (Jn. 2:19-21; Eph. 2:15; Col. 1:22; Heb. 10:10; I Pet. 2:24; 3:18; 4:1).

In fact, I Peter 3:18 plainly says: *"For Christ also has once suffered for sins, the just for the unjust, that He might bring us to God, being put to death in the flesh, but quickened by the Spirit."* *"Put to death in the flesh,"* plainly tells us that He only died physically and not spiritually.

## THE JESUS DIED SPIRITUALLY DOCTRINE

This doctrine claims that Jesus Christ became a sinner on the Cross (actually taking upon Himself the nature of Satan) and died and went to hell (speaking of the burning side of the pit), where He suffered there for three days and nights. During that time, Satan and his cohorts laughed in hellish glee because in their minds, Jesus was defeated. At the end of that three days and nights, God then said, "It is enough." At that time, they continue to say, Jesus was born again, becoming the first born of many brethren. This means that He had to be born again as any sinner is born again, that is, if they are to be saved. He was then resurrected from the dead.

That's the reason that this teaching claims that the Cross was the greatest defeat in human history; consequently, they will not sing songs about the Cross or the blood in their churches.

There are many things wrong with these statements, but

the main problem is (as we have said some paragraphs back), it is pure fiction from beginning to end. In other words, you won't find this tale in the Bible.

As far as I know, this doctrine that Jesus died spiritually is believed by all the adherents of the Word of Faith message.

Every cult and pseudo-Christian sect disparages the Cross and/or the person of Christ. An enemy of the Cross is one who even suggests that the sacrifice of Christ on the Cross was insufficient for salvation. Anyone who disparages the Cross is teaching another gospel, and the destiny of such teachers is destruction (Phil. 3:19). Therefore, we must come to the conclusion that no enemy of the Cross can be a brother in Christ.

## WHAT DID HAPPEN FROM THE CROSS TO THE THRONE?

The Bible portrays two things that Jesus did when He died on the Cross of Calvary.

First of all, Jesus went down into the heart of the earth, where He preached to the fallen angels.

The Scripture says: *"By which also He went* (between the time of His death and resurrection) *and preached* (announced something) *unto the spirits in prison* (does not refer to humans, but rather to fallen angels; humans in the Bible are never referred to in this particular manner; these were probably the fallen angels who tried to corrupt the human race by cohabiting with women [II Pet. 2:4;

Jude, Vss. 6-7]; these fallen angels are still locked up in this underworld prison);

*"Which sometime* (in times past) *were disobedient* (this was shortly before the flood), *when once the longsuffering of God waited in the days of Noah* (refers to this eruption of fallen angels with women taking place at the time of Noah; this was probably a hundred or so years before the flood), *while the ark was a preparing* (these fallen angels were committing this particular sin while the ark was being made ready, however long it took; the Scripture doesn't say!), *wherein few, that is, eight souls were saved by water.* (This doesn't refer to being saved from sin. They were saved from drowning in the flood by being in the ark.)" (I Pet. 3:19-20).

Second, immediately after His death on the Cross, our Lord delivered all the souls who were in paradise and took them with Him to heaven.

The Scripture says concerning this:

*"Wherefore He said* (Ps. 68:18), *When He ascended up on high* (the ascension), *He led captivity captive* (liberated the souls in paradise; before the Cross, despite being believers, they were still held captive by Satan because the blood of bulls and goats could not take away the sin debt; but when Jesus died on the Cross, the sin debt was paid, and now He makes all of these His captives), *and gave gifts unto men* (these 'gifts' include all the attributes of Christ, all made possible by the Cross.)

*"(Now that He ascended* (mission completed), *what is it but that He also descended first into the lower parts*

*of the earth?* (Immediately before His ascension to glory, which would be done in total triumph, He first went down into paradise to deliver all the believing souls in that region, which He did!)" (Eph. 4:8-9). That place is now empty.

Now when a believer dies, his soul and spirit instantly go to be with Jesus (Phil. 1:23).

The only things that the Bible mentions that Jesus did during the three days and nights that He was in the heart of the earth after His death on Calvary were:

- Preach to the fallen angels in prison.
- Deliver all of the Old Testament souls who were in paradise.

## ENEMIES OF THE CROSS

Paul said, *"Brethren, be followers together of me* (be 'fellow imitators'), *and mark them which walk so as you have us for an example* (observe intently).

*"(For many walk* (speaks of those attempting to live for God outside of the victory and rudiments of the Cross of Christ), *of whom I have told you often, and now tell you even weeping* (this is a most serious matter), *that they are the enemies of the Cross of Christ* (those who do not look exclusively to the Cross of Christ must be labeled 'enemies'):

*"Whose end is destruction* (if the Cross is ignored, and continues to be ignored, the loss of the soul is the only ultimate conclusion), *whose god is their belly* (refers to those who attempt to pervert the gospel for their own personal

gain), *and whose glory is in their shame* (the material things they seek, God labels as 'shame'), *who mind earthly things)"* (Phil. 3:17-19).

## THROUGH THE BLOOD OF HIS CROSS

Paul said, *"And, having made peace through the blood of His Cross, by Him to reconcile all things unto Himself; by Him, I say, whether they be things in earth, or things in heaven"* (Col. 1:20).

He then said, *"In whom we have redemption through His blood, even the forgiveness of sins"* (Col. 1:14).

Then the great apostle said, *"But God forbid that I should glory, save in the Cross of our Lord Jesus Christ, by whom the world is crucified unto me, and I unto the world"* (Gal. 6:14).

## THAT WE MAY HAVE BOLDNESS
## IN THE DAY OF JUDGMENT

The heading refers to the coming judgment seat of Christ (I Cor. 3:11-15).

There will be no unredeemed at the judgment seat of Christ, with their judgment taking place at the great white throne over a thousand years later (Rev. 20:11-15).

At the judgment seat of Christ, motives and works will be judged. If it's works tendered by the effort of trying to produce faith, that will be judged very negatively. If it's works as a result of faith, which is the right way, then motives will be judged.

If our faith is properly placed in the Cross of Christ and not at all in ourselves, we have boldness now, even as we will have boldness then. The way it's translated in the King James makes it seem as if it is boldness we will come by on that coming day; however, the Greek text puts it in the present:

*"We have boldness and connection with the day of judgment. We are looking forward to that day and the fact that on that day we shall stand before God.*

*"Incidentally, the judgment seat of Christ will have nothing to do with the penalty of sin for the simple reason that this was taken care of at the Cross. And yet, wrongs toward fellow brothers and sisters in the Lord, which have never been settled, will have to be settled at the judgment seat of Christ."*

If our faith is totally in the Cross of Christ, then we have boldness now even as we will have boldness then. This refers to our basing our lives totally and completely on what Jesus did there for us and not at all on ourselves. In other words, even as John will say in the next verse, there will be no fear. However, let the reader understand that this boldness of which John speaks is predicated totally and completely on the finished work of Christ and our faith in that great sacrifice.

## BECAUSE AS HE IS, SO ARE WE IN THIS WORLD

The heading refers to the Christlike life. This makes the

saint like Christ as he dwells in the midst of a world of sinful people, and at the judgment seat of Christ, the Lord Jesus will not condemn those who were like Him while they lived on earth.

As He stands before the throne of God in the glory, Christ represents the believer while yet in the world. All that He is in the sinless perfection of His nature is the property of the believer, who can, therefore, say: *"Thus I stand before God! There is no fear in love; but perfect love casts out fear: because fear has torment. He who fears is not made perfect in love"* (I Jn. 4:18).

## THERE IS NO FEAR IN LOVE

The heading speaks not of a godly fear, which is scriptural and right, but rather a slavish fear.

The idea is that if we love God as we ought to, our love is not diluted. Proper love at the same time demands proper faith. In other words, it's impossible for a believer to properly love the Lord if that believer does not properly exhibit faith in the Lord also. When we speak of faith, we are speaking of the Cross.

This means that if our faith is not properly placed in the Cross, but rather other things, our faith is improper and will translate into improper love, which will translate into fear.

The love of which John speaks here is not known by the poor results of its action in man, but rather its perfect action in God, and that perfection manifested itself at Calvary.

This perfect love is a fact, and it manifested itself outside of man in order for the salvation of man.

The believer knows it by the gift of God's Son, and he enjoys it by the gift of God's Spirit. It is at Calvary that we learn what love is and that when we had no love for God, God loved us perfectly, though we were far from Him and dead in sins.

Man has no love for God, and I speak of unredeemed man; his pretention to possess it is self-deception. He cannot find it by searching within himself, but he can know it as manifested in the atoning sacrifice of Christ. He gave the life that loves and made propitiation for sins.

Those who really possess this divine nature love because they are loved. It is especially a fraternal love. It loves fellow-believers more intimately than the nearest relatives who are unconverted. It binds the heart with a stronger bond to persons never seen than to the dearest companions of childhood: It is a new nature, a realm outside of natural human affection — a realm of divine love. It is a fellowship with God and with all who know Him. There is, in truth, no love outside of that realm.

## BUT PERFECT LOVE CASTS OUT FEAR

The heading presents the fact that love and fear are incompatible. They cannot coexist. For the Christian, love is first an experience of the Father's love for us. This love is so powerful and life changing that when we know it, we are forever removed from fear. That's quite a statement!

As we have stated, the fear spoken of here is not to be confused with reverence for God. Reverence will only deepen through the experience of God's love. The experience of the holiness of God's love makes us desire to be even more obedient to His commands, but it also removes us from the power of fear.

Whatever may take place in this world cannot nullify the power of His love or separate us from it. Similarly, if we experience fear in any portion of our lives, to that extent we deny God's love and fail to trust Him.

Going back to the previous verse, fear is the opposite of boldness. Where the one is, the other is not. The love of God, which translates into the sacrifice of Christ, has removed all our sins (I Jn. 1:9; 2:1-2; 4:10). What is there left to make us afraid?

## BECAUSE FEAR HAS TORMENT

The heading probably should have been translated, "Because fear has punishment."

John states this in order to show why, with it being brought to its goal, God's love necessarily throws out all such fear. This love would not reach its proper goal without that.

Punishment from God should have no place in the thinking of the Christian, with Christ having suffered in our stead. If the believer fears punishment from God, this means a believer does not really understand the Cross and what

Jesus did there.

Now, of course, this doesn't mean that we can trifle with the Word of God. Anyone who takes lightly the Word of God will suffer its consequences.

However, if sin has been committed, it must be confessed before the Lord and forsaken. With that being the case, there is no fear of punishment, for Jesus took all of that at the Cross. While there definitely may be chastisement from the Lord and, in fact, always is, that is, if we are truly children of God, this is not to be looked at as punishment. It is rather to be looked at as correction, which is altogether different from punishment. Punishment is for the mere purpose of inflicting pain, while chastisement is correction in the sense of bringing us to the right way.

## HE WHO FEARS IS NOT MADE PERFECT IN LOVE

The heading presents such a statement that always and without exception, it translates back to the Cross.

Perfect love always centers up on the Cross. This was the perfect demonstration of God's love for man and demonstrated itself accordingly. In the first place, this type of love must originate with God and is, therefore, perfect because God doesn't have anything less than perfection.

As we have stated, this perfect love is not demonstrated by the poor results of its action in man but by its perfect action in God. We continue to speak of the Cross.

Consequently, the only way the believer can evidence

this perfect love is by loving the One who is perfect, namely the Lord, and understanding what He has done for us in the realm of Calvary. As it centers up in the Cross, at the same time, of course, it centers up in Jesus.

If we do not properly understand the Cross, then we are not made perfect in love. If we properly understand the Cross and place our faith and trust in that finished work, of necessity, the love of God will then be generated in our hearts, and that love is perfect, i.e., made perfect.

To be made perfect involves a process, which again refers to our faith in the sacrifice of Christ.

When we talk about loving God, we must understand that we can only do such through a proper understanding of His Son, the Lord Jesus Christ, and what He did for us in the sacrifice of Himself. Placing our faith totally and completely in that finished work, at the same time makes perfect the love of God within our hearts, which drives out all fear.

*"We love Him, because He first loved us"* (I Jn. 4:19).

## WE LOVE HIM

The short phrase, *"We love Him,"* proclaims that which comes only after He has first loved us.

Love must never be conceived as a natural experience of the natural man. There is a natural love, but it must not be confused with the divine love (agape). The love John speaks of originates with the Father. It became manifest in and through the Son and now characterizes the lives of the children of God. Therefore, he begins this summary by saying, *"We love."*

Although the Greek verb form expresses either exultation or description, here it is better to understand it descriptively: as the Father loves and as the Son loves, so also will we love.

The love with which we love is not our own. We do not create it, and neither do we even have the power to express it. It is always God's love or Jesus' love in us. However, because we abide in the Father and the Son, the love becomes also our own love. It is not that God reveals His love apart from us or in spite of us, but that He invites us to love even as He loves. So we return to Him His own love and love Him with a gift of His love.

If we truly love Him, there won't be any fear there, or depression, or discouragement.

*Down at the Cross where my Saviour died,*
*Down where for cleansing from sin I cried,*
*There to my heart was the blood applied,*
*Glory to His name.*

# SELECTED BIBLIOGRAPHY

**CHAPTER 5**

George Williams, *William's Complete Bible Commentary*, Grand Rapids,
    Kregel Publications, 1994, Pg. 688.

**CHAPTER 8**

George Williams, *William's Complete Bible Commentary*, Grand Rapids,
    Kregel Publications, 1994 , Pg. 878.

Ibid.

# ABOUT EVANGELIST JIMMY SWAGGART

The Rev. Jimmy Swaggart is a Pentecostal evangelist whose anointed preaching and teaching has drawn multitudes to the Cross of Christ since 1955.

As an author, he has written more than 50 books, commentaries, study guides, and The Expositor's Study Bible, which has sold more than 2 million copies.

As an award-winning musician and singer, Brother Swaggart has recorded more than 50 gospel albums and sold nearly 16 million recordings worldwide.

For six decades, Brother Swaggart has channeled his preaching and music ministry through multiple media venues including print, radio, television and the Internet.

In 2010, Jimmy Swaggart Ministries launched its own cable channel, SonLife Broadcasting Network, which airs 24 hours a day to a potential viewing audience of more than 1 billion people around the globe.

Brother Swaggart also pastors Family Worship Center in Baton Rouge, Louisiana, the church home and headquarters of Jimmy Swaggart Ministries.

Jimmy Swaggart Ministries materials can be found at **www.jsm.org**.